Abe's Story

A Holocaust Memoir

by Abram Korn

Edited by Joseph Korn
Annotated by Richard Voyles

Longstreet Press
Atlanta, Georgia

Published by
LONGSTREET PRESS, INC.
A subsidiary of Cox Newspapers,
A division of Cox Enterprises, Inc.
2140 Newmarket Parkway
Suite 118
Marietta, GA 30067

Printed in Canada
1st printing 1995
Library of Congress Catalog Card Number: 94-74226
ISBN 1-56352-206-3

Cover design by Jeff Cohen .
Book design by Neil Hollingsworth
Film preparation by Advertising Technologies, Inc., Atlanta, Georgia
Original maps and endsheet illustration by William Fahnoe. The endsheet illustration is a composite drawing after images in several photographs from the archives of Yad Vashem in Jerusalem and the YIVO Institute for Jewish Studies in New York.
Cover photo: The Korn family several years before World War II. (Abram Korn is the small boy highlighted on the right.)

I dedicate this book to my wife, Ellie, who inspired me through the years to succeed in all my undertakings. I also dedicate this book to the memory of Mr. Jack Y. Platzblatt. I came to America as a displaced person. I wanted to succeed in life through my own individual efforts and not from the charity of others. Mr. Platzblatt gave me the opportunity to do just that. I wrote this book because I am proud to be an American. I want to show my own children and whoever reads this book why I feel so grateful to be part of this great country, the United States of America.

Contents

Editor's Note

My father left a rough first draft of his memoirs when he died in 1972. Based on thorough research and interviews, I have smoothed some of the wording, corrected minor factual errors, and filled out several stories. Every effort has been made to maintain my father's language, flow of thought, and sentence structure to ensure that *Abe's Story* accurately reflects his thoughts, experiences, and record of the Holocaust.

Some of the names have been changed to protect privacy, but most names have been left just as my father spelled them, in hopes that I will hear from some of my father's friends or relatives.

Acknowledgments

Many people helped along the way in the process of preparing my father's story for publication. First, I'd like to thank my editor, Suzanne Comer Bell. After I had worked for many months to get my father's rough draft into publishable form, Suzanne painstakingly compared the latest version to the original manuscript, paragraph by paragraph, and diligently worked to restore many of the original words that she felt were "too precious" to leave out. She treated my project with the respect it deserved and is just what I was praying for as an editor. Suzanne is a true purist. Thank you, Suzanne.

I am eternally grateful to Jack Wyland, may his memory live forever, and to Rabbi Benjamin Rosayn, who encouraged and helped my father to get his story down on paper. Thanks also to Jack Wyland's family.

I want to thank William and Elizabeth Schweitzer, may they rest in peace, who brought my parents to America from Germany. And thanks to the rest of the Schweitzer family.

I especially want to thank Mr. Jack and Aggie Platzblatt, my godparents, who gave my parents the opportunity to build a new life for themselves and for our family. They both added so much love to our lives. I want to thank my parents, Abe and Ellie, who instilled the values of family in me, my brother, Jack, and my sister, Helen. May the memories of my parents and godparents live forever.

Mary Lou Helmly worked so hard to decipher the original handwritten notes and typed the original manuscript. Penny Lewis and Shirley Fleeman helped to retype the original manuscript. Years later, Katerina Malin and Sharon Galloway carefully entered it into my computer.

It was Elie Wiesel's encouragement through the years that gave me the resolve to have my father's story published. His able assistant, Martha Hauptman, always saw to it that he got my messages, even when he was on sabbatical and I just "had" to reach him.

Thanks to Martin Gilbert for the excellent documentation

in his books on the Holocaust, through which I was able to verify several important aspects of my father's story.

My father's cousin, Miriam Kleinman, and her husband, Eli, helped me locate survivors who knew my father and helped identify old photographs. Miriam also provided a useful description of Lipno, Poland. Eva and Leon Kruger, Ann and Herszel Menche, Joe Grosnacht, and Simek Kirstein all helped with stories about rebuilding their lives in postwar Germany.

I would like to thank all my students through the years, who always encouraged me to have my father's story published.

Rabbi Jordan Parr, Rabbi Avigdor Slatus, and Rabbi Maynard Hyman all contributed in various ways.

Longtime friend Gary Capelouto has encouraged my efforts from the very beginning. Thanks also to his wife, Susanna, who has been working with me to produce the public radio/television documentaries on my work with my father's book.

Many thanks to Janet Bray, who volunteered much of her valuable time to help with the preparatory editing.

Thanks to Debbie Gillespie, who was inspired to create some beautiful artwork for us after she read my father's story.

Special thanks to Esther Levine, who introduced me to my editor at Longstreet Press.

Thanks to the staff of Longstreet, who have been wonderful to work with and have allowed me to be closely involved in the publishing process.

Many friends read the manuscript and/or gave their input, suggestions, and support. Among them are Greg Godek, Kevin Ryerson, Dan Poynter, John Stoessinger, Barry Steinberg, Jerry Blumberg, Thomas Welling, Tim Gillespie, Kenny Shusterman, Myra Scheer, Henry and Donna Sheer, Cary and Sarah Friedman, Diane and Lionel Solursh, Marc Solursh, Frank and Laurie Chambless, Diane Van Giesen Barrett, Jim Anderson, Daniel McLeod, Harold Mays, Frances Sideman, Rick Davis, Randy Salzman, Ingrid Heggoy, Milton Butler,

Acknowledgments

Norman Prinsky, Annie Alpert, Deborah Day, Debra Bennett, Linda Lynch, Eric Fleishner, Ina and Valarie Spratlin, Frederic Beil, Nancy Sladky, Eve-Lyn Forbes, Alexa Selph, Cheryl Zimmerman, Heide Lange, Hilda Rubin, Barbara Steinberg Smalley, Abram Serotta, Betty Cantor, Barbara Lance, Rob Bissell, Michael Berger, Joe Beck, Chris Kelly, Dottie Schmidt, Blanche Selwyn, and my dear mother-in-law, Carol Myers.

Finally, I would like to thank my beloved wife, Jill (my editor #1), who helped and encouraged me every step of the way, and my wonderful children, Jason, Jana, and Julia, who gave me all the more reason to have my father's story published.

Introduction

Holocaust survivors are special to me. As a Holocaust educator to students and other teachers, I have heard many survivors tell their stories. Some give their accounts on video, some on television, some in books, some in person—and each always has an impact on me. My students seem just as drawn to these survivors. On course evaluations almost everyone comments on the survivor's story: "He should have come sooner"; "I will never forget her story"; "Keep bringing survivors in to speak"; "I couldn't put his book down; I read it in one night." Few fail to speak of the powerful presence of the survivor. Presence, not so much in body, but simply in being alive, right before us. That presence has a power that says, this person has a story to tell because he or she *lived*. This person survived a system designed for his or her destruction.

Abram Korn was such a survivor. Through his memoir, *Abe's Story*, he tells the story of his life in Lipno, Poland. As a 16-year-old boy working at his father's lumber business, Abe had the usual aspirations of a teenage youth: romance, education, responsibility. However, Abe's life from 16 to 22 was anything but normal, after the Nazis occupied Poland and began rounding up Jews. Instead of romance Abe found himself in a ghetto. Instead of education Abe learned how to make one day's portion of bread last for three. Instead of responsibility Abe lived under the demoralizing cruelty of abusive *Kapos* and guards. For nearly six years, Abe suffered in the clutches of the Nazi machinery. Almost two years of these he spent in Auschwitz, one of the deadliest concentration camps. Yet Abram Korn survived. . . .

The Nazis entered Abe's life in September 1, 1939, destroying his world like a tidal wave destroys a harbor. They swept in with a dark overarching power, crashing down with a devastating force, leaving in their wake splintered pieces of once whole and happy lives. This devastating force was the product of years of Nazi practice on German Jews. Hitler, once becoming chancellor of Germany on January 30, 1933, acted swiftly against German Jews. One week after he was given power on March 24 to enact laws on behalf of the Reichstag (German Parliament), Hitler declared a one-day boycott of all Jewish-owned stores and businesses in Germany. Following the boycott, on April 7, 1933, all Jews working in the government were ordered to retire.

The Nazis wanted to force every Jew out of Germany, and it seemed as though there was little to stop them. The Nuremberg Laws, passed on September 15, 1935, deprived all Jews of any rights as citizens in Germany. Property, businesses, and homes were taken away from Jews and handed over to Germans. In the name of overcrowding, Jewish children were no longer allowed to go to their classrooms. And Jewish doctors were not allowed to treat German patients.

Many Jews tried to leave Germany, and the attention of the international community came to focus on their plight. On July 5, 1938, these international leaders held a conference in Evian, France, to address the problem of the growing number of refugees. Many countries had restrictive immigration quotas set for Jews, and if they could not be increased or lifted, Jews would have no place to go when they left Germany. Unfortunately, these nations, including the United States, felt it would be impossible to change their immigration restrictions, leaving thousands of Jews stranded in Germany.

It seems Hitler read their action as permission to continue his aggressive policies against Jews, concluding that nobody would come to their aid. And on the night of November 9 of that same year, 1938, Jewish-owned stores and businesses were broken into and robbed in a statewide pogrom known as Kristallnacht, the Night of Broken Glass. All across Germany, the Nazis burned and destroyed synagogues, desecrated Torah scrolls, and beat rabbis, while local police stood by and looked on. Jewish homes were broken into and family valuables were thrown out of windows onto the streets and burned. And the next morning nearly 30,000 Jewish men were arrested and sent to concentration camps Dachau, Buchenwald, and Sachsenhausen. Some children were never to see their fathers again.

Introduction

By September 1939, the tidal wave of Nazi hatred for Jews was a force backed by state legislation and state enforcement. When it crossed the border into Poland it rushed in, washing away any sense of human dignity for Polish Jews. All the policies and practices which took years to implement in Germany were employed immediately in Poland. Therefore the devastation came quickly for Abe and his family as people in his community, children he had played with, all seemed to turn against them overnight. Abe and his family were forced to wear yellow arm bands identifying them at all times as Jews. Their lumber business was confiscated, and by the spring of 1940 they were forced from their home into the Kutno Ghetto.

Abe's Story tells of one young man's struggle against the Nazi's dehumanizing system. With relentless precision the Nazis stripped their prisoners of dignity and life, yet Abe never fully relinquished his dignity to them. Abe continued to treat himself and those around him as human beings. When other prisoners were humiliated in their fight to live, Abe strove to help them maintain their humanity. Rather than condemn people for their actions, he anguished when humanity was lost—whether in Germans, Poles, Russians, or Jews.

The Nazis were bent on taking everything away from the Jews of Europe. When it was all over, they had taken away from Abe not only six years of his life, but his mother, father, and his two sisters as well. The Nazis had a plan, a "Final Solution," and this plan included no survivors. They failed.

Abe survived . . . and tells his inspiring story.

Richard Voyles

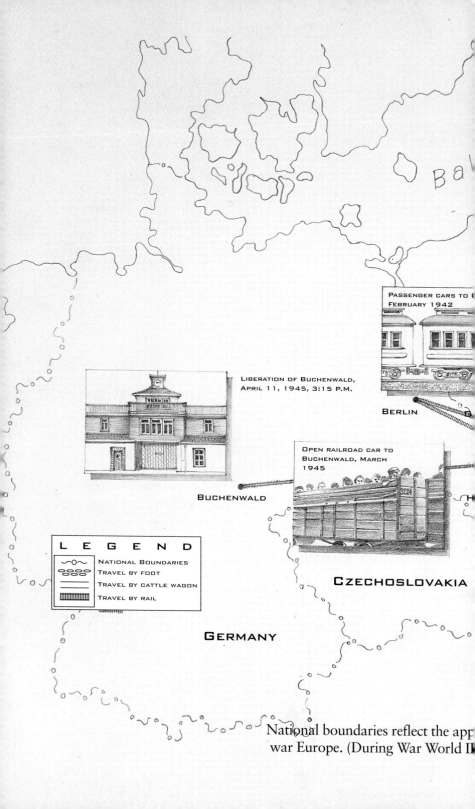

PASSENGER CARS TO
FEBRUARY 1942

BERLIN

LIBERATION OF BUCHENWALD,
APRIL 11, 1945, 3:15 P.M.

OPEN RAILROAD CAR TO
BUCHENWALD, MARCH
1945

BUCHENWALD

CZECHOSLOVAKIA

L E G E N D

NATIONAL BOUNDARIES
TRAVEL BY FOOT
TRAVEL BY CATTLE WAGON
TRAVEL BY RAIL

GERMANY

National boundaries reflect the app
war Europe. (During War World I

CART TO
OSTROWY,
EARLY WINTER
1939

EXPLORING
THE KUTNO GHETTO,
WINTER 1939

LIPNO

POLAND

POSNAN
(HARDT)

OSTROWY

KROSNIEWICE

KUTNO

GARFINGAL
AND ABE WALKING TO
KROSNIEWICE, LATE FALL 1940

CATTLE CARS TO CAMPS
HARDT, GROSS-ROSEN, AND AUSCHWITZ

AUSCHWITZ/BIRKENAU,
APRIL 1943-
JANUARY 1945

OSWIECIM
(AUSCHWITZ/BIRKENAU)

THE DEATH MARCH,
LATE JANUARY-MARCH
1945

political divisions of pre- and post-
this region was Greater Germany.)

The Beginning

My story begins in 1939 when I was 16 years old. Air raid sirens and church bells woke us in the night, tolling the danger and destruction at the hands of Hitler's air force, the *Luftwaffe*. So war minded were these pilots, they destroyed a group of covered wagons, not knowing—or caring—that they contained simple building materials for our town's railroad station.

It was September 1, 1939, the first day of what is now referred to as World War II. Even though the number of injured in this initial attack was relatively small, the bombing foreshadowed a war that would destroy millions of people and would touch uncounted lives with misery.

Our family lived in Lipno, Poland, a city of approximately 30,000 people, near Warsaw. Many people called Lipno a "little Paris." Parks and gardens highlighted the city, surrounded by beautiful forests. My father, Joseph, ran our small lumberyard on the outskirts of town, handed down to us from my mother's parents. I remember many hours of playing in the stacks of lumber, climbing, hiding, and running with my sisters, my friends, and my loyal dog, Kajtek. Kajtek was my faithful companion for many years.

We were a close-knit family, with much to live for. My father was a deeply religious man and was proud of his Jewish heritage. He was the first son in a line of descendants of the Gerer Hassidim, an esteemed dynasty in the Hasidic Jewish movement of Eastern Europe. He loved his family dearly and was a leader in our community. My mother, Hannah, was a strong woman who devoted herself to our family. At 16 years old, I was learning the family business and helping my parents to support our family. My sisters were younger than I. Gitel was 13, and Mirjam was 10. Gitel was a very sensitive and beautiful girl, with long, dark hair and brown eyes. She had an angel's face and loved to dress up in colorful clothes. Mirjam was also beautiful and was mature beyond her years. She was strong willed and fiercely independent. Mirjam was driven in everything she did. We had a happy life in our beautiful community, and felt that nothing could ever change that—until the attack by the *Luftwaffe*.

The events of that night terrified us all. The surprise attack left our townspeople bewildered, awaiting news and preparing for the worst. After three days, the city officials announced that all males, from the ages of 16 to 55, were to assemble at Wloclawek, a city about 20 miles away. The Polish Defense Forces planned to give up Lipno and make a stand against the invading Germans at Wloclawek. They made no plans for the women, children, and property, naively assuming that the Germans would not really harm them. They reasoned that, in war, only the combatants typically engage in hostilities, sparing the civilian population.

In response to this order, my father and I packed our few most necessary belongings and tied them onto our prized bicycle. We walked alongside our bike on the evacuation road. There were hundreds of other stunned people, traveling with their wagons, their cattle, and on foot. After a two-day journey, walking and occasionally hitching onto a moving wagon, we found ourselves at the outskirts of Wloclawek. We were exhausted, hungry, and confused. We had to cross the Wisla River Bridge to enter the city.

We now had to find food and shelter. My father and I sought out distant relatives in Wloclawek, who offered us shelter. Time worked against us, however. In less than a week, we had completely exhausted our food supply. We spent all our money on bread, and we soon found ourselves on the public bread line. The starving waited for hours for their quota of bread. Getting bread was serious business. While we were waiting, the *Luftwaffe*

Abe was 15 years old in this 1938 photograph, the last surviving image of him as a carefree child before the war.

The Korn family several years before World War II. On the front row, Abe is the second child from the right.

This image of Joseph Korn, Abe's father, was created from his picture in the family portrait.

Gitel Korn, the older of Abe's two sisters, wearing a Warszawianka, the official costume of Warsaw worn during local celebrations and festivals.

aimed their bullets at us—but none would run for shelter. What would have been the good of escaping one threat to life when the threat of starvation was equally as real? Food meant life, and bread was our only food.

Our plans for survival were now being methodically threatened. The Polish Defense Forces dynamited the Wisla River Bridge to stop the German advance, but the German military outsmarted us. They sent their tanks, armor, and men to attack through the land route and easily gained control of the city.

For the Jewish people, it seemed an unusual coincidence that the Nazis entered Wloclawek on the first day of the Jewish New Year—one of the High Holy Days—Rosh Hashanah.

Despite the obvious danger, my young friends and I were eager to see German soldiers up close, with our own eyes. We found them to be young, well dressed, and polite. In our innocence, we could not imagine that these well-mannered people would harm us. Not recognizing us as Jews, the soldiers spoke freely to us. Sad and frightening news emerged. When we were able to speak person to person to the German soldiers, they told us that they planned no harm for the Christian citizens of Poland, but they had no desire to do anything but harm to the Jews. Not recognizing us as Jewish Poles, the German soldiers could not discern a Jewish Pole from a Christian Pole.

Evil decrees and news came rapidly. In less than a week, the Nazis ordered all Jewish citizens of Wloclawek to register with the authorities. My father and I read this notice posted in the town square. It gave us some insight into what was to come. We decided to return to Lipno. After all, we were in Wloclawek by order of the Polish Defense Forces to protect our homeland, but Lipno was our home. A ferry was in operation to cross the Wisla River, in place of the destroyed bridge. From there we trudged our way back home.

Helplessness and disaster stared us in the face. My father, an active, robust member of the community, was in the prime of his life at 39 years old. My father, who had always supported us through his lumber business, and walked the earth with earned dignity, now realized that he could no longer protect his family or himself—and I saw him, a big, strong man whom I loved and respected, simply break down and cry.

We arrived home and it was like heaven seeing our family again. My mother fed us leftovers from the holiday feast that we had missed. We rested and feared the unknown tomorrow.

Our fears were not in vain. After two days, the Germans had identified and recorded the names of the Jews in Lipno. They ordered us to wear distinctive yellow arm bands, called *Judenstern* (Jewish star), displaying the six-pointed Star of David. To humiliate us even more, the Nazis ordered every Jew to remove his hat and get off the sidewalk when approaching a German in uniform. They considered us unfit to walk with human beings. We were just beasts of burden.[1]

Then the Nazis announced that Jews could not possess any animals that might be used for food or transportation. The only exceptions were dogs; they categorized Jews and dogs together.

The noose began to tighten. The Nazis claimed that the Catholic majority had persecuted and discriminated against Lutheran Poles of German descent. They identified these German Poles and elevated them to positions in the citizens' militia. Previously, no one had been able to distinguish them from other Poles. The Nazis also took advantage of anti-Jewish sentiment prevalent throughout Europe. They had a plan, and used everyone who would willingly collaborate.

The Nazis used Jewish property and money to their advantage. The next move, one of many, was to divest the Jews of all property, which the Nazis then confiscated.[2] Of course, many tried to hold on to whatever they thought they could get away with. Jews could no longer be businessmen, nor could they serve

1. The practice of forcing Jews to wear a badge, setting them out from the rest of the population, began in Christian Europe in 1215, when the Fourth Lateran Council mandated that Jews must wear a badge on their clothing. Fifty-two years later, Roman Catholic leaders decided at the Synod of Breslau (1267) that Jews must live in designated ghettos. For centuries Christian thinkers and leaders saw the Jews as responsible for the death of Jesus and therefore as enemies of God and humanity to be either converted, expelled, or killed.
2. This Nazi practice, called "Aryanization of Jewish property," was amended to the Nuremberg Laws (September 1935) in June of 1938. While the Nuremberg Laws stripped Jews of individual civil rights, this amendment made it legal for the state to confiscate Jewish businesses.

in any professional field.[3]

It did not take long for the German occupiers to confiscate our business. One morning they arrived with a convoy of horse-drawn wagons and carted our entire stock of lumber away. We had questions, but the only answer we got was a receipt. We were not alone. The Nazis also confiscated other small lumberyards in the area.

One day our cousin, who owned a small fabric and piece-goods store, gave me a small rug. I was delighted, but he was being neither generous nor considerate. He knew that the German Occupation Forces would soon confiscate everything. Since there was a strict curfew imposed, I waited until it was permissible to walk the streets before I tried to carry it home. My luck was not good. Janke, a former employee and friend of ours, spotted me and the rug. He was now in full Polish-German military uniform. Since this man had made a living at our lumberyard for years, I assumed he would let me continue on my way. I was wrong. He grabbed me as he would a common criminal and made me march to my house.

When my frail mother opened the door and saw me, the rug, and Janke with fingers on his gun, she immediately understood the situation. She knelt before him, crying, and pleaded, "Please take the rug and leave my son alone." Janke took the rug and left me with my mother. He could have accused me of stealing German property or of any other crime he might invent.[4]

To make light of the frightening incident, my father told us a story about some people riding on a train. One passenger owed 25 *zloty* (about $5 U.S.) to his traveling companion. The train soon halted unusually between stops. Surmising that robbers had stopped the train, the debtor said to his friend, "Here are the 25 *zloty* I owe you." After a few minutes, the robbers opened the train compartment and took all the passengers' money. Either way, he would have been out the 25 *zloty*. This way, he

3. In April 1933, four months following Hitler's appointment as chancellor, laws were passed making it impossible for Jews to have jobs as civil servants, lawyers, or doctors.
4. With all civil rights denied to them by the Nuremberg Laws, Jews were without protection from the court systems or police. Without the ability to have someone arrested for hurting them, Jews became easy targets for beatings and murders.

also paid off his debt.

The Nazis used Jewish labor from the start. They ordered all Jewish males between the ages of 14 and 55 to work two days each week for the German Occupation Forces. My first assignment was to clean up a school that the Nazis used as offices. The Nazis told us they would pay us later for our labor. When the day was over, they divided the work crews into groups, lined us up, and escorted us to various rooms, supposedly to collect our wages. The Germans had a preconceived plan. Our wages consisted of a powerful beating. Some of the Nazis were ashamed by their comrades' deceptive, ugly actions. These very few Germans tried to salve their consciences by throwing candy and cigarettes to us, but we let their great gifts lie on the floor. With heads bowed, bodies in pain, and hearts broken, we made our way slowly home.

The Nazis later assigned some of us to the waterworks. They had destroyed our electricity supply and had demolished the pumps that forced the water into holding tanks. We had to haul the water in buckets to the holding tanks by hand. This was backbreaking work. My cousin, who suffered from tuberculosis, was in our work crew. He would collapse often under the strain. The Nazis would revive him with a pail of water tossed in his face, and a threat of worse punishment to come. He and I plodded along.

Among the Germans were some with human feelings, values, and emotions. Captain Schmidt was one of these good people. When he learned that I could speak German, he asked me to be his guide through the city. We walked and talked like human beings for many hours. He told me about his family, and I told him about mine. I showed him the beautiful parks and the quaint, terraced homes. Our tour took us to the outskirts of Lipno. When I pointed out our modest home and lumberyard, Captain Schmidt asked to meet my family. I escorted him in and introduced them to each other.

After greeting my mother, Captain Schmidt let his eyes run over and inspect the spotlessness and charm of our modest home. In Germany, he had been taught that all Jews were filthy and infested with parasites. Posters on walls everywhere had illustrated Jews with large, hooked noses and faces like pigs. He could see that these were all lies. Captain Schmidt felt at home in our house; it reminded him of his own home. He returned many times to visit and talk with my parents, at great risk to his career as a Nazi officer, and perhaps at risk to his life. Even in all the evil, there were still good people. The exception is always present, even among the Nazis.

Soon, the Nazis ordered Jewish males to bring all articles containing gold to a specified place, where the commandant, or chief Nazi officer, would explain what we must do to be able to live as citizens of the community. We knew that to disobey could mean death, but some still tried to hold on to their possessions.

After we deposited our golden trinkets, the commandant let us know, clearly, that the Jews were the guilty ones. "You Jews are responsible for the war," he told us, "and you must pay the war's expenses. We will use all your gold to help us win the war. If you are still hiding any gold, you do so at the risk of death to yourself and your loved ones. Don't take this risk." He paused a few moments to see if anyone would come forward with more valuables. No one did.

"Now, when I count to three," he barked, "you better disappear quickly." Perhaps a few quick-footed ones did run fast enough to escape the beating that followed. Polish-German militiamen, called *Hilfspolizei*, surrounded the marketplace. These former neighbors of ours delighted themselves by swinging their sticks and whips on our Jewish bodies.

The Jews were not the only ones to suffer. The Nazis' research staff came up with a list of priests and all others who could be in a position of influence or leadership in the community, including our mayor. They picked them up, without warning, and shipped them to an unknown destination. (We had no idea at the time, but we later assumed that the Nazis must have sent them to a concentration camp.)[5]

The Jews, however, were still the favorite target of the Nazis.

5. Concentration camps were built all over Germany. The first camp was erected near Dachau in March 1933. As Nazi power and reach increased, so did the number of concentration camps: Sachsenhausen in September 1936, Buchenwald in August 1937, Flossenburg and Mauthausen in 1938, and Ravensbruck, a women's camp, in May 1939. Detained in these camps was anyone considered an opponent of the regime: socialists, clergy of various faiths, people considered to be "asocial" (such as homosexuals, prostitutes, and beggars), and those considered to be members of "inferior races" such as Jews and Gypsies.

The Nazis ordered all Jews to assemble on Tuesday—it seems that they liked Tuesdays for doing their worst dirty work—ready to travel to a distant place. They told us to pack a second change of clothing for better assembly and assured us that we could keep our clothing. Not to heed this order meant instant death.

When we assembled, the Nazis told us that many Germans were cold and needed clothing. This was the signal for the many militiamen to take our packages of clothes from us. We could do nothing if we wanted to live. My father was standing next to me, carrying his best and warmest fur-lined coat. A young German militiaman, attracted by this coat, approached my father. On coming closer, we recognized him as Fritz Janke, a former employee at our lumberyard. (He wasn't the same Janke who took the rug.) Fritz reached a noble high point of character—he wanted to let my father keep his overcoat. He called out in a frightened voice, "Lice! Lice! A coat with lice! Get away from me with your lice!" No one would come near him, and so he helped my father keep his coat.

Moments later, the Nazis announced that, at the count of three, we were to flee as though a thousand devils were kicking us. I fortunately eluded the militiamen, who had their clubs prepared to strike. Looking back, however, I saw my father being beaten on the head. As I turned to help, I heard him trying to reason with his tormentor. "Why do you want to hurt me?" he cried out. "You know I would have done you nothing but good!"

In my youthful exuberance, I yelled to my Daddy and said, "Dad, don't try to appeal to his mind or conscience. He hasn't any!" The Nazi stopped beating my father and took off after me, as I ran in circles to escape. He fell in the mud, but his whistles summoned the help of a dozen men. They caught me and beat me over my head. Being small, I slinked within my coat and escaped some of their blows. On my back was a bundle in which my mother had placed a large jar of honey for me to have during my journey. Their blows cracked the jar and, in the dark, they probably mistook the dripping honey for my blood. They dropped me and walked away, expecting me to bleed to death.

Leaving Home

In times of danger and risk, one's ears and mind become sharp and receptive. We learned that in about two weeks the German Occupation Forces planned to force all Jews out of Lipno and into the Warsaw Ghetto. We did not relish the thought and made plans to escape this sad fate. My parents and I were people of faith and looked forward to the day when this madness would pass, when we could return to our home and the community we loved.

My father planned to go to my grandparents' summer home in Ostrowy. He hired a driver and wagon to haul our family, while I remained at home to arrange storage for our few possessions until after the war. This was not an easy task. Most of our Christian friends were too frightened even to talk to me. To help Jews at this time was dangerous, but I did find a few friends who were willing to accept some of our furniture.

I approached our friend and neighbor Mr. Pytelewsky, who used to hire me to help him in his work as an electrician. He agreed to store some of our belongings, but word somehow reached the Nazis, and they decided to make an example of him. The Nazis not only confiscated all of our belongings from Mr. Pytelewsky, but they also took property from many of his Christian friends. Then the Nazis publicly whipped Mr. Pytelewsky, with his family and neighbors watching, and jailed him for several months.

Trouble makes one grow up and mature ahead of his years. The Nazis soon dynamited the local synagogue, and we were all now convinced that the Germans fully meant to make

Lipno *Judenrein*—without Jews—forever. I was 16 years old when I found that I could not discharge my responsibility—to find storage and refuge for the balance of our belongings. Leaving one's home and birthplace is never easy, but I knew that leave it I must.

I decided to head for Ostrowy to join my parents. Getting out of the city was not an easy feat for a Jew. I took my bicycle, a package of food, and my loyal dog, Kajtek. Very few Jews dared to travel by bicycle after the war began, especially with a dog. I removed my arm band, pretending to be a Christian with no curfew to abide by. It was a dangerous plan, but it had to succeed because I had no other choice. It was either the frying pan or the fire. To wear my *Judenstern* invited the hostility of all; not to wear it risked punishment by the German Occupation Forces. I left at about 8:00 P.M., after curfew for Jews. The militiamen patrolling the streets let me pass. No doubt they assumed I was the son of one of their own, going on a short trip.

The night was dark, cold, and windy, with clouds threatening rain. After two hours of traveling, the rain began to fall. To make matters worse, my bicycle light went out. The rain had now penetrated my outer clothing, and I was shivering in the cold. The fear of the unknown made me feel sad, lonely, and afraid. Despite this, I did not lose my balance. I decided to find shelter for the night and try again tomorrow.

In the distance I could see the edge of a village, Chelmice. I headed toward the first light I could see. After slowly navigating my way in the dark, I found myself at the entrance to a home. I knocked on the door, while my shivering dog barked alongside. I could hear conversation in German from within the home. I was standing at the entrance of a Polish-German home. It was cruel luck, I thought, but it was even more dangerous to run away.

The door slowly opened, and the lady of the house asked me my wishes: "What do you want?" she asked in Polish. I replied in Polish, "I am in need of lodging for myself and my dog. We are on our way home to Ostrowy, and the broken light on my bicycle forced us to stop our journey." The lady was very polite, but refused me lodging. She took pity on me, standing there wet and shivering from the cold, and advised me to seek lodging at the fourth house slightly ahead on the right.

Slowly, I approached the fourth house. It was a large shack and a poor home with windows boarded and no lights visible. My knock on the door brought forth frightened voices. "Who is there?" I thought this time that my luck had changed for the better. They were speaking Yiddish!

The kerosene lamps shone brightly inside, as the head of the household asked me in Polish, "What do you want?"

In Polish, I replied, "I need a night's lodging and a hot meal. I will pay for both." They allowed me to enter their one-room house. Again I heard whispers in Yiddish, giving me courage to reveal my Jewish identity.

Their attitude changed immediately to one of welcoming a member of their own family, and they greeted me warmly. They had heard of my fine family, and they gave me every courtesy. As my clothes dried beside the hearth, Kajtek and I ate a bowl of hot soup. They gave me a choice place to sleep, where I rested with my dog cuddled up beside me. In the dark, my dog's growls and other noises soon awakened me. The mice and rats appeared as soon as the light was turned out! I could not wait until morning to continue my journey.

There were so few Jews in this village that the Nazis treated all the townspeople as Poles. They had drafted my hosts' son, Moshe, into the German Military Civil Patrol. It was Moshe's turn to patrol the streets the following morning, and he advised me to leave at 6:00 A.M. I thanked my hosts for their hospitality. Tears came to our eyes, and I took my leave to the unknown road ahead, hoping to reach my parents and family in Ostrowy later that day.

The rising sun saw me continue my journey. After an hour, my dog, my bicycle, and I arrived at the outskirts of Wloclawek. The Wisla River Bridge had still not been repaired. It was a simple thing to pay one's fare and cross on the ferry—but not for Jews.

I still wasn't wearing the required arm band identifying me as a Jew. My heart thumped with fear as I paid my fare, boarded the ferry, and crossed the river with my dog. Our troubles did not end there. Armed German *Wehrmacht,* or members of the German army, stood at street corners along the way, spot-checking and searching passersby. Appearing as a Polish teenager with bicycle and dog, I was able to go unmolested by these Nazi soldiers. My courage and deception had paid off.

Several hours later, I found myself on the road outside a small town, Lubien. Some of my relatives lived there, and I was tempted to stop. Tired and hungry, with Ostrowy still two hours away, I pushed on with my second breath to be with my parents.

My dog, who had been faithfully trailing me, was on the verge of collapse. Luckily, a horse-drawn hay wagon appeared. I begged the farmer to allow me to rest my dog on the hay, and he agreed. Exhausted though he was, Kajtek was not content to sit comfortably unless I at least held onto the rear post of the wagon. Kajtek loved me and would have forsaken comfort to be by my side.

The minutes, hours, and kilometers brought us closer to my parents' home of refuge. The sun was setting, and I had been trudging wearily all day long. The thought that I would soon be standing in the presence of my loving parents cheered me and kept me on my path. The moment arrived and I walked in, unannounced, to the dwelling place my parents now called home. All joy exploded as my parents, my sisters, and I joined in a heavenlike reunion. Kajtek broke all bounds of control. He ran in circles, jumped for joy, and licked every member of the family in happy disbelief.

Kajtek and I had not eaten all day long. The ordinary plate of hot soup tasted like a royal feast. After I answered my parents' many questions, they kissed me goodnight, and I fell into a deep sleep.

The warmth of our family reunion soon turned into a chilling nightmare. Some militiamen, who were former neighbors of my uncle, appeared the next morning under orders to evict us. They gave us fifteen minutes to gather our belongings. Along with our frightened relatives, we climbed aboard the cattle wagons waiting outside.

My thoughts turned to my dog, my prized possession. I grabbed him to take him with me. Without a word or show of feeling, without heart, a German soldier yanked Kajtek away from me, and as my dog rolled in an effort to stand up, he was shot dead before our eyes. The wagons sadly began their dark journey. My sisters and I tried to bring courage and light to our parents by singing "Hatikvah"—the song of hope. All we had left was hope.[1]

Throughout the day, the moments ticked slowly away. The fear of the unknown was heavy among us. About two hours later, the cattle wagons on which we were hauled arrived at their destination. We were ordered off the wagons and into a large warehouse that had previously been used as storage by a sugar factory. We all guessed correctly; we were in the city of Kutno. The Germans had placed fifty other Jews there before our arrival.[2]

Soon, a German SS guard announced that we were to wait for instructions from the *Sturm Führer*, the officer in charge. We waited anxiously and fearfully, not knowing what catastrophe awaited us. After more than an hour, we heard two rifle shots. We then heard cracks of a whip, and screams of its victim. Seconds later, the *Sturm Führer* entered with a grand display of military pomp. A hush fell over us as we waited to hear what he had to say.

"Dear friends," he began, "the shots you heard were the executions of two Jews who disobeyed our orders. The whipping was for a lesser crime. If you want to continue to live with your families, you must do exactly as we tell you. We will soon take you to a comfortable lodging place for your own good and protection. A special section of town is being set up for your use. You can live and work there with your fellow Jews in peace."

The *Sturm Führer* then pointed to large tables on which were two large, empty boxes. "Place all of your money in this box," he said, "and in the other, all of your other valuables. You may keep your watches, as you must be on time for everything you are ordered to do. You will be searched periodically. If we

1. While Abe mourned the death of Kajtek, his dog, wondering how these people could be so cruel, the Nazis had begun their euthanasia program. This program led to the death of more than 70,000 mentally and physically disabled people, including children.
2. The fall of 1939 saw the systematic roundup of Jews from rural communities in western Poland into designated ghettos. By the end of January 1940, some 78,000 Polish Jews had been driven out of their homes.

find any valuables on you whatsoever, you will be shot on the spot." The *Sturm Führer* then walked out of the room, but we had the feeling that the Nazis were spying on us to ensure that we followed orders.

"We will do exactly as we are told," our parents said to us. "We don't want to risk losing our lives for the sake of some money and a few valuables. If we all live," they said, "we will have many opportunities to replace whatever we have lost."

Several minutes passed, and the *Sturm Führer* returned. He looked at the collection of money and valuables with satisfaction. He ordered the guards to gather it up, then turned around and left.

The guards told us to find our quarters, but there were no quarters in this warehouse. There were no beds and no facilities for people to live. Nevertheless, we made do with our corner in a large room that was about 75 feet square. We unrolled the blankets and pillows we had grabbed on short notice, unpacked the rest of our belongings, and, with choked voices and wet eyes, called this our home.

We later learned from other Jews who had preceded us that the Nazis had forcibly taken one of them, who was innocent of any wrongdoing, and purposely whipped him to scare us all. He required more than one week to recover. The Nazis had also fired the rifle shots into the air just to frighten us.

My sisters and I were young and curious. We left our parents' security to go outside and snoop around to find out where we were. A sad sight greeted our young eyes. All around us, we could see a high wall and a gate patrolled by armed German SS men. We were in a walled-in ghetto or prison. We realized that our freedom was gone and that our lives were in great jeopardy.

The Ghetto

The next day, wearing his yellow arm band, the head of the Jewish community told us that we were among the first of many Jews to suffer forced homelessness. The Nazis ordered the entire Jewish community of Kutno, more than 300 families, to make their own move into this compound. Slowly, without interruption, our room filled with other Jews from Kutno. The crowding was indescribable, and facilities were practically nonexistent. More than 2,000 people shared only one toilet, actually an open pit, and there was only one hand pump for drawing water. We had to wait in line for hours.[1]

Somehow, the Jews from Kutno obtained some used lumber and erected privies—better described as raw outhouses. For their use we were charged an admission fee, which most of us could not afford because of our empty pockets.

The Jewish lay-leaders, the *Yeddishe Gemeinde*, began to bring some order out of chaos. Selected as liaisons by the Germans, the *Gemeinde* organized a *Judenrat*, or Jewish ghetto government. The *Judenrat* consisted of twenty-four members of the community. The Nazis issued all orders through these councils. The council members were then responsible to see that we obeyed these orders. In this way, the Germans could get the most for the least effort.

The *Gemeinde* set up a kitchen and gave us one hot meal in the afternoon and a slice of bread with jelly in the morning and evening. When we were lucky, we could have margarine

---

1. The Nazis intended for the overcrowding and the poor sanitary conditions within the ghettos to increase the spread of disease.

or butter on our bread instead of jelly. Soon the *Gemeinde* set up a post office and an office for the paymaster.

The Jewish people from Kutno, knowing the conditions in the ghetto in advance, were more able to prepare for it. They brought small potbellied stoves with them. They located their quarters by the walls, where they made holes to vent the stoves. Like camping, housekeeping began.

Every day we hoped, by a miracle, that this nightmare would end, that we would be back in our own homes. Until that day arrived, we knew we had to improvise to exist at all. We found scraps of wood for the stove and purchased tea on the black market. We concocted a makeshift Sabbath feast, with only soup and tea. Life went on despite its impossibilities.

Each morning, we had work details supervised by German civilians. We had the worst kind of work to do, such as repairing the railroad, unloading coal, and cleaning the streets. We also had to clean the German soldiers' quarters so they would glisten and shine. To turn us into a willing work force, the Nazis systematically broke our bodies and spirits.

I shall long remember my return to our "factory home" after my first day of shoveling coal. My face was black with coal dust, my clothes soaked with sweat, and my body disfigured with pain and exhaustion. With tears streaming down her mellow face, my mother embraced me, even though coal dust covered me from head to foot. She kissed me on my blackened forehead and patted my back, saying, "My wonderful little breadwinner! My wonderful little breadwinner!" I was more than rewarded for my backbreaking and heartbreaking experience.

"Work Makes Life Sweet," the Nazis mockingly told us verbally and on posters. To keep us from despair and to avoid rebellion, they paid us two *Marks* per day (about 50¢) through the *Gemeinde*. Sometimes we worked outside the confines of the ghetto and could buy food to smuggle back inside.

Although shoveling coal was neither easy nor desirable, an idea soon came to me. If I could somehow bring in a little coal, we could exchange it for other necessities, like food or soap. The Germans had to give us a little food to keep their labor force alive, but gave us no soap at all.[2]

I slowly befriended a German guard. Taking a chance, perhaps with my life, I asked him, "Please, please, please, can I bring in some coal when returning from work each day? My family doesn't have enough coal to keep warm, and we could also trade it for food. You know we don't have enough food to eat."

He was sympathetic. "How are you going to carry this coal?" he asked. "It will look too obvious if you put it in your pockets."

"Each day," I told him, "I could hide some in my underclothing. A little coal each day would help us more than you could ever know."

"But remember," he said, looking at me with pity, "I do not see you. If you are caught, you are on your own." The penalty for theft was death.

I considered myself lucky, especially when my father began working with me. It gave us a double opportunity. For nearly a month we stole and brought in as much coal as we could conceal.

One evening, when my father and I returned from work, my sisters and mother were waiting, all aglow. We guessed that something good had probably happened—but what? My mother kept her secret until she could tell us in private.

"A miracle has happened!" she finally exclaimed. "Months ago, Gitel sewed a 100 *zloty* bill [about $20 U.S.] in her underclothes against an emergency which she felt would certainly come. Because of the tension and fear, she forgot all about it. She even forgot to give it up when our lives were at stake in disobeying the *Sturm Führer*. With this money, we can buy at least twenty loaves of bread!" This was more bread than we received from the Nazis for our family of five for more than forty days. It was a God-sent miracle. We rejoiced in the knowledge that we had some good fortune to anticipate.

In March 1940, when winter's grip had loosened, they finally moved us into the Kutno Ghetto from the temporary compound.[3] It took about two months for a large segment of the

2. The food supply, controlled by the Nazis, was intentionally not enough to keep people alive.
3. Just days before Abe and his family were moved into the Kutno Ghetto, orders were issued to set up a concentration camp at Auschwitz, Poland.

Jewish working force to arrive. Things happened that will always stand out in my memory.[4]

We soon had evidence that our lay-leaders were defrauding us. We knew that we were not getting our fair share of pay for our strenuous work. We could think of no other solution than to overthrow the *Judenrat*.

For two weeks, two of us planned a rebellion. When the day for action finally arrived, we followed our plans to the letter. Within ten minutes, we had bound and gagged the guilty ones. The Jewish Safety Patrols, armed with police clubs to keep order, turned against their own Jewish superiors and helped us to overthrow them. They knew what we were doing was just and necessary. My assignment was to replace the man in charge of our post office, a big job for a 17-year-old. All the ghetto prisoners cheered the overthrowing group for our heroic deeds.

Our success, though long in planning, was short-lived. The Nazi guards suspected something during a routine check. They hastily investigated and found us in the position of taking over. "We have no complaint with the Germans," my friend, Yakob, and I explained to a Nazi officer. "We realize that you treat us well and pay us well for our labor," we told him cleverly, "but our own leaders are stealing much of our hard-earned money. We had to do something about it."

"If this is the case," said the officer, "we will not punish you, but you must return the *Gemeinde* to their appointed positions of leadership." This we did as commanded. Our revolt lasted about three hours.

Despite these tense moments during our inner rebellion, things soon quieted down. For the sake of keeping our sanity, we established a routine and tried to make the best of our sad situation. Always we hoped and hoped that things would turn out all right—that things would get better—that the nightmare

4. On June 16, 1940, the roundup of Jews into the Kutno Ghetto was complete, leaving the Jews permanently enclosed. At Lodz, less than 40 miles away, the ghetto was "sealed" on May 1, 1940; Warsaw, some 70 miles away from Kutno, was "sealed" on November 15, 1940.

would fade away.

While we waited and hoped, we tried to build a sense of community in our ghetto.[5] We organized a library, of sorts. Everyone who had a book gladly donated it. We even had a librarian, Chaim Lopotik, the gifted son of our beloved musical cantor. Like his father, Reb Joseph, Chaim excelled in many areas. He composed original songs—words and music—and taught them to our youth group, keeping our spirits as high as possible. In our despair, Chaim shed light and joy, though temporarily, and dispelled the darkness.

Every Friday night at our *Judenstadt* (our Jewish home away from home), we gathered to usher in the Holy Sabbath. We looked forward to these moments of prayer and togetherness. Our common troubles welded us into a cooperative community. On Saturday nights, the young people—I among them—would find a clearing in the field inside the camp where we gathered regularly. The program consisted of a review and discussion of various books and ideas. Our meetings always opened and closed with songs of hope for a future life of normality with freedom and cheer. Our songs were in Hebrew, Yiddish, and Polish. We could not easily forget our mother tongue, Polish. Most of our conversations were still in Polish.

Our Saturday night youth programs and get-togethers strengthened many friendships and sparked romances, even for me. A slender, shapely, dark-eyed jewel shone for me. Her name was Golda Schuster. As her name implied, I saw her as a golden beacon that radiated through my days and nights.

One afternoon, the *Gemeinde* transferred me from the coal yards to a new job with the railroad "bowl gang," repairing the cross ties and pinning the tracks. My 5'4", 90-pound frame wasn't built for this kind of work, but they expected me to keep up with the others. Late one afternoon, after hours of exhausting work beyond my endurance, I collapsed, and a track section fell on my right foot. By a miracle, my small foot did not break, but swelled to double its size. My friends carried me back to the ghetto and laid me on my blanket on the floor.

---

5. While the Jews of Kutno waited and hoped, on June 22, 1940, France lost the war with Germany and Nazi occupation began.

News spread, and Golda was among the first to react. Within minutes, she was kneeling on the floor and placing cold compresses on my swollen, aching foot. She had taken the time, before coming to my aid, to change her clothes. Wearing white, she resembled a private nurse as she took care of me.

Golda's eyes clouded with tears, looking at me with love and sympathy. It seemed that she also wished, by some miracle, that we could both run away from this ugly place to a setting where pain, poverty, and humiliation were no more, to a place where we could live, laugh, and love. With eager tenderness, her skilled, healing hands sought to alleviate my pain. My parents knew of Golda and respected our privacy. They left us alone, knowing that I was in caring hands.

None of us can choose our parents or destiny. Golda was the daughter of a simple shoemaker. In her own right she excelled, but the tradition of family *Yichus* would come into play against us. I was the first son in a line of descendants of the *Gerer Hassidim*, an esteemed dynasty in the Hasidic Jewish movement. I was only to associate with girls of equal *Yichus*, or status. Even within the dark walls of the ghetto, where we should have been on an all-for-one and one-for-all status, *Yichus* played an important role and was a weighty factor. How foolish it was, yet I was bound by the force of this family tradition.

Within the hour, the scene was to change. My uncle, Yankel, had heard the news. He had to do something about the family *Yichus*. He felt that it was a family shame to have a shoemaker's daughter so close to one of our family elite. "Why, this girl is unworthy!" he exclaimed. My uncle felt that he had to get a replacement for Golda. He dispatched his own daughter, Zonka, who had inherited her father's disposition.

Zonka very rudely told Golda off and sent her sobbing into the night. "Who do you think you are," she shouted, "playing up to Abe? I know better ways of helping him and I am taking over!"

This episode broke our hearts. Golda could not endure the forced separation that now faced us, and she made plans to escape with a friend. On the following day, she succeeded in putting miles between us.

Zonka's smiles were false. Her sympathy was false. Zonka came only because, like her father, she relished the satisfaction of stomping on another under the guise of righteousness. She had left me in less than an hour, never to return. Sagelike, she played her deceptive part well. My loving mother took care of me for the next three weeks.

Even within the walls of the dismal ghetto, many tried to improve their lot. My sisters were no exception. They had both been taught by my mother to keep house, to sew, to knit, and to crochet. They could turn their talents into money, as our family was always hungry. They bought up old woolen sweaters that were no longer usable, and slowly, meticulously, they unraveled the ragged sweaters into balls of wool. They used the wool to knit new sweaters to sell, and they knitted day and night, even in the dark. With the extra money they earned, our family bought food to sustain our bodies.

But evil lurks even among the suffering and their fellow sufferers. Mrs. Kabtzan, a ghetto neighbor, made a deal with my sisters after hearing of their fine work. They agreed to make a new sweater for her from the remnants of three old ones. Both girls spent the next three weeks knitting the sweater, as specified by Mrs. Kabtzan. The finished sweater was a masterpiece of design and beauty. The following afternoon, Gitel delivered the finished sweater with pride to Mrs. Kabtzan and waited for the money that they had so honestly earned.

Mrs. Kabtzan placed the sweater on some makeshift scales and, without even looking Gitel in the eye, refused any payment to my sisters. "I gave you exactly three pounds and two ounces of wool," she grimaced, "but now my new sweater weighs only two pounds and six ounces. You stole my wool, and I will pay you not one *zloty*." The miserly Mrs. Kabtzan conveniently forgot that when unraveling an old sweater, much of the wool falls away unusable.

Gitel, who was shy and sensitive by nature, could never argue with or talk back to another. Heartbroken, with tears on her face, she ran home and related her tale of woe. My mother cried sympathetically. My father became righteously indignant and yelled in anger, "This is not right!" as he pounded his fists to emphasize the point.

Into this scene of bewilderment and inaction, my youngest sister commandingly came forward. Mirjam was certainly kind, but she was one who would always stand up and fight for her rights. She assured everyone that she would personally take care of things in her own way, that no one needed to worry. Without waiting for discussion, Mirjam packed her night clothes and headed out. With much self-assurance, my 11-year-old sister strutted into Mrs. Kabtzan's quarters. "I am here to live with you until you pay us what you owe us!" Mirjam said as she began to make herself at home.

Some neighbors came to hear the reason for the disturbance. Mirjam convincingly related the injustices done loudly enough for the neighbors to hear and agree. Fearing the accusations and disrespect being heaped on her, Mrs. Kabtzan hurriedly paid Mirjam for the work. With a smile of satisfaction, Mirjam came home. She stood with pride as she placed the money in our mother's hands. We all slept well that night and were certainly proud of little Mirjam. With this money, we could buy seven loaves of bread. How happy this made us!

Our Final Farewell

The cool of autumn followed the heat of summer. In late 1940, the cold winter winds began blowing. An ill wind it was. We had almost completely exhausted our supply of wood. Every scrap, every limb, every wooden particle was burned to keep warm. Human excretion and garbage accumulated and overflowed. The stench, the lice came. Our undernourished bodies had a battle to wage—against an outbreak of typhus.

Life in the ghetto now revolved around an unending routine of waiting in line. We still had only one toilet and one water pump to serve the needs of about 2,000 imprisoned Jews. I remember waiting in the long, long line for my turn to get water for my family. As I reached the pump handle, I looked behind into the faces of those waiting. Their trembling hands and emaciated feet supported weak bodies less than half alive. With this sight registering in my mind, I could not help but to remain there for them, pumping water for those who could no longer pump for themselves. After some time, my mother would send one of my sisters for me, and we would go home.

As soon as I rested my water bucket, I had to queue up in another line for our small ration of bread and soup. It was a three-hour wait, and waiting in the cold wind with a weakened body was a life-supping task. My sisters and I took turns in line so we could rest under shelter without losing our place.

As we had dreaded, a typhus epidemic came to visit and stay at our ghetto. Despite our many requests, the German Occupation Forces were now too tired and bitterly inhuman to remove the waste and sewage or even to permit us to do it. Typhus was the inevitable result.

The Nazis no longer allowed anyone out of the ghetto, and no one was foolish enough to come in. Previously we could work, under tight security, outside the confines of the ghetto. We could use some of the *grosze* (coins) that we earned to buy extra food and smuggle it back into the ghetto. Now this had all ended. We either had to get food by waiting in line or not eat. Our fate and battle with imminent death were closing in on us, even as the gates of the ghetto locked us in.

Typhus is an especially ugly, painful, and frightening disease, but a quick way to die. Spread by lice, it causes high fevers and a severe cough, and it completely debilitates the body. On Tuesday I spoke to Schloma and Faibel; on Wednesday they were both dead. Fear and helplessness spread along with dark dismal death. Young and old died for nothing. They died because of man's inhumanity.

Within the ghetto, four Jewish doctors had improvised a hospital, which was no hospital at all. There were no facilities, no medicine, no stethoscopes—nothing except makeshift beds and the doctors' dedicated wills to help and to heal. Within hours, the eighteen beds quickly filled with the living who were dying. Others had no choice but to die at "home," and it made little difference.

Still, the lines seemed endless. One either waited and waited for bread, for water, for toilet facilities . . . or waited in line to be buried. Such disaster brings out the best, the worst, and the dark humor in people. The sight shocked our teacher, Reb Mottel. Over and over and over again he would say, "You see this line for bread . . . people want to be first. You see that line of the dying and the dead . . . people want to be last!" Such was his lament.

The Jewish people revere even the lifeless remains of a person. After all, the Holy One gives life, and he takes it away. The Society of Holy Endeavor, Hevra Kadeesha, now had more to do than it could handle. Its main task was to prepare bodies properly for a dignified burial. Despite the distress, danger, and lack of supplies, the society functioned. Its members carefully placed the bodies on a wagon and pulled them out to the burial grounds. They reverently placed them in marked graves and intoned the proper prayers over them.

Doom stared us in the face. Our only hope for survival was to escape—if our feet were able to carry us. But how? Some of the German guards had a spark of pity left. If we could offer some inducement to compensate them for their risk, we could possibly arrange to escape.

I learned that a friend of mine, Garfingal, was planning to escape. He was skilled in these matters and had the proper connections to find out what it would take for me to escape with him.

Sadly, I had little to bargain with for escape outside the wall. All I had was a wristwatch and a throw rug which my had sisters hooked from the remains of sugar sacks. It was pretty and unusual.

The next morning, Garfingal brought me good news. His contact would be on guard duty from midnight until 6:00 A.M. At about 4:00 A.M., I would be able to barter the watch and rug for my life. Of course, I could be bartering for death at the hands of another Nazi guard who might observe our escape. Even my friend's contact, who agreed to blink for a price, might turn on us. There was no guarantee. I gave him the watch and the rug with which to make the arrangements.

Even more trying than facing death itself was facing my parents and sisters with the news that I was planning to escape. I shall never forget my mother, sobbing and saying to me, "Son mine, Abe, listen to me! Do you think that you are any different or better than us? Don't act in this selfish way. You should want to stay with your family and share the same fate with us. What will befall us will, with God's will, befall you too. Don't be selfish. Don't desert your family." My mother convinced almost everyone that she was right—even me.

My father had the courage to think differently and logically. After reflecting on the problem that confronted us all, he said, "Do you want Abe to stay here and die, God forbid, with us? Or would you rather he escape and live—and possibly help us later to escape and live also!" My father's wisdom prevailed and convinced us all that escape was the right thing to do.

Without waiting for calm or normality, we immediately put our nervous energy to good use. My mother placed my one pair of underwear, a towel, a shirt, socks, and a pair of trousers into a rucksack. This was my only luggage. My father, who had been following the events without participating, now broke the silence and reminded me to pray often, and to remember—I had somehow forgotten to take my best pair of shoes with leather soles that I had been saving. I thankfully took them from him and hurriedly placed them inside my pack.

Now my family stared into empty space with me, waiting for the zero hour—when I was to attempt my escape. My father was calm and collected, despite the tension that gripped us all. "Don't forget to remove your Jewish star insignia from your coat," he said. Even though they displayed our revered Star of David, these yellow badges of shame identified us easily to any German, even from a distance, as Jews to be abused.

My heart broke as the moment of departure and separation from my family neared. I ran to meet the outstretched arms of my mother. Her frail, weakened form convulsed with sobs as she embraced me and kissed me good-bye. She held on to me with a grip that expressed volumes. It said, "Go." It said, "Stay." It said, "How sad." It said, "How much I love you, now and forever." It said, "God, please watch over my son." It said the unspeakable. It spoke of a mother's love for her only son. My sisters cried and held on to me as if to hold on to the memory of this moment—and to life.

My father—who had always been my strength and shield—waited until last to come over. He had a rugged face with a simple, short mustache and a head of premature gray, born of pain. He removed his pinch spectacles, fell on my shoulder, hugged me with all his might, then abruptly let go. "Don't ever forget us," he said. "Don't ever forget who you are and what our religion teaches us. Watch yourself, and may the Eternal, who watches over all of us, mercifully protect you." I had to summon all my strength to make my feet take me away. I was never to see my family again.

The German guard had received my watch and throw rug, as well as a bribe for Garfingal to escape with me. He let us out, and we breathed the cold but free air. We were grateful to be outside the wall with a new chance for freedom—and for life. As we headed for Krosniewice, our prime consideration was to avoid being apprehended by the Nazis.

We rehearsed what we would say if stopped. I had an old identification card that I had received in Ostrowy, showing that I was a resident there. My companion, Garfingal, had no identification whatsoever. He planned to claim that he was a refugee from Warsaw and that we had met in Ostrowy. He would say that we had decided to look for a job in Kutno, but had failed to find employment, and were now returning to Ostrowy.

Krosniewice, a small town between Kutno and Ostrowy, was about 15 kilometers away. We learned that it had an open ghetto—a poor section of town where all Jews from the city and surrounding areas were forced to live, with some freedom to come and go. They lived in overcrowded houses, but they did live in houses. There still was not enough to eat. Life was difficult but not impossible. We had no choice but to make this our destination.

We walked with fear and trepidation and prayer. We heard our hearts beating. Miraculously, we arrived at the outskirts of Krosniewice without being detected. Garfingal would continue on to Gostynin, where he would stay with relatives. We wished each other luck and parted. My father's and mother's relatives lived in Krosniewice. On their help did I pin my hope.

Healing Angels

At only 17 years old, I faced the task of building a new life for myself, while still trying to help my family. I had nothing to help me get started but my own inner resources, my will to live, and the help of others. My future was uncertain, but at least I had a future.

My mind now focused on the most immediate problem that lay before me—where to stay. My Aunt Chaya and her two daughters, Sarah and Rachel, were now also strangers in Krosniewice, having been sent there from Lipno. They were the burdensome guests of their kin, Mrs. Rose Issac and her family. I decided to risk rejection and ask to live with my aunt and her daughters. Even though their quarters were small and exceptionally poverty stricken, the choice of asking to live with my father's family, in a larger house, frightened me. I felt like a stranger among them.

Mrs. Issac allowed me to share the quarters with my aunt. I slept on four chairs pushed together, next to the kitchen table. For comfort, I had a few rags to soften the hard wooden seats and several blanket remnants for a cover. Even so, Mrs. Issac's son, Eizik, resented me. They could, after all, charge someone else to stay there who could afford to pay rent.

On the following day, I paid a courtesy call on my father's brother, Shaaye-Schloime. I told him of the dreaded living conditions at the Kutno Ghetto and how terrified we all were. He was pleased that none of us had fallen victim to typhus, as so many others had. My uncle was delighted to see me, but never invited me to stay with him.

Very quickly thereafter, I became part of the routine. All Jews in Krosniewice had to register with the *Gemeinde*. The Germans required that every Jew give two days of free labor to the German Occupation Forces. I learned that the local Jews still had their belongings, including money, and that some would rather pay off another than do their allotted burdensome and demeaning work. After working my required days, I worked as many extra days as I could to earn extra money.

The Nazis caught on to this scheme quickly and formalized the system, thereby profiting from the situation. The *Gemeinde* soon had to meet a quota of 66 laborers per day. They taxed those who would not or could not work, assessing them 5 *zlotys* per day (about $1 U.S.). The *Gemeinde*, in turn, paid 4 *zlotys* per day to those willing to work extra days. There was always a longer line of willing workers than there were extra *zlotys*.

Luck shone on me. Mrs. Rose Issac worked directly with the *Gemeinde*. Despite my small build, she managed to select me regularly for work on my free days. I used some of this extra money to help with Aunt Chaya's expenses, thereby helping Mrs. Issac as well.

The young people were not eager to stay in their crowded quarters. We sought out other young people with whom to spend some of our evenings. I will never forget my friend, Abram Danziger, to whom I could pour out my aching heart. Abram was a young man of 18, who knew all the local young people. We would walk and talk, share our inward thoughts, and encourage one another.

One evening, Abram introduced me to Ester Rosenthal, the local watchmaker's beautiful daughter. Whenever I looked at Ester and saw her shapely figure, my heart would skip a beat or two. Her creamy white complexion was set off by her beautiful dark eyes and hair.

In my own inexperience, however, I could find no suitable way (or courage) to express my feelings for her—but love will find a way. One evening, after a hard day's work, I lined up with everyone else to buy my loaf of bread. I had been waiting for more than two hours in the seemingly endless line. Everyone needed food, and this was our only opportunity to buy it. We waited and hoped that there would still be bread to buy when we reached the bread window.

Into my empty life and aching heart, now appeared Ester. Her loveliness overcame me—but what was I to do? An inspiration came to me. "Ester," I yelled, "here is the place where you were standing." Ester surveyed the long, long line that loomed ahead. Not to have to take her place at the end of it delighted her. Her beautiful face shone with joy as she glided over and took her place in front of me. Ester bent toward me in loving appreciation. She smiled and thanked me in her low, vibrant voice. My insides stirred, and I felt that we had finally begun to connect.

Ester's smile was soon to turn to mourning. The Germans had given her father, the local Jewish watchmaker, some of their broken watches to repair. They had confiscated most of these watches from Jews, who purposely gave them their broken watches. The Germans ordered him to repair the watches by the following week. Unfortunately, he could not repair many of them by the deadline because parts were not available. This was the only excuse the Nazis needed. They killed Ester's father, and took all his watches, tools and equipment. She was devastated by her father's death.

I continued to do extra work for the *Gemeinde*. Most of my money went to my favorite charity—my parents and sisters, whom I had never for a moment forgotten. Their faces haunted me bittersweetly. I was able to buy food on the black market and have it smuggled into the ghetto. There is always a black market in hard times, thriving on the needs and wants of the affected. Each Wednesday, a covered wagon, camouflaged with hay, would make a trip from Krosniewice to the Kutno Ghetto with supplies. All it took was money or valuables to pay for food and clothing, which are everyone's primary needs. My friend, Racheal Rottenberg, was the personal maid for the Kutno Ghetto commandant. Through her, perhaps, even the commandant had an ounce of pity. He allowed the camouflaged wagon, with food and clothing, inside the ghetto walls, but Racheal did have to pay him one-third of her collections.

What a wonderful feeling it was for me to know that, even from afar, I could help my parents and sisters. If they had enough to eat, their bodies might have enough resistance to fight off the typhus epidemic. During the weeks that followed, I worked as hard as I could to buy and send food to my loving family.

Racheal soon came back to Krosniewice on a purchasing trip. She had collected many valuables and some money from the weak, starving survivors of the Kutno Ghetto to buy some food for them on the black market. She walked into our quarters and asked for help carrying the goods back to Kutno.

"What would you pay me to help you?" I asked.

"One dozen eggs and a pound of butter," she replied.

I could not help but take on this dangerous job. I carefully wrapped her bundles of food in some cloth. I leaned forward to steady this heavy burden on my back and walked the 15 kilometers to Kutno. Knowing that my family would receive extra food to nourish them was sufficient reward for my risk. I thought that I had found the key to survival.

The following week, I set out on another dangerous, but well-paying journey. And dangerous it was. Several kilometers outside Kutno, two gendarmes (policemen) stopped me. They took my precious cargo of food and interrogated me in their wagon. My friend, Racheal, had taken a separate path and fortunately avoided capture. I knew what awaited me and decided that, come what may, I would not divulge any real names, even of dealers in the black market.

It did not take long before the gendarmes caught another Jew. They hauled him onto the carriage and continued toward Kutno. On the way, the gendarmes decided to have some fun. Life was dull for them, and a Jew could always provide a little diversion. They threw us off the wagon and commanded us to run alongside the horses. To make certain we ran, they whipped us twice as much as the horses. After we fell from exhaustion, they stopped the carriage and told us to climb into the back. I now heard the Austrian gendarme tell his German counterpart that he would like us to run alongside the horses again—that it was great fun for them and good punishment for the Jews. The German driver objected to this idea but the Austrian insisted, so once more they threw us off the carriage, whipped us and made us run with the two horses. We soon collapsed again. Once more, we somehow pulled ourselves aboard the carriage and lay down, hoping to die.

When the gendarmes arrived in Kutno, they did some shopping and then headed toward the Krosniewice gendarme station. Again, they interrogated me and, again, I told the same story: "I bought the food on the black market from strangers in Krosniewice, and I was carrying it to Kutno for sale at a profit."

The six-foot-tall gendarme quickly grabbed me and tossed me onto a long bench. He straddled the bench, with my head between his knees, and held my hands. The other one began lashing me with a whip. "Tell us the full truth, or we will whip you to death!" they repeated to me. I held out in silence and passed out from the ordeal. In a semiconscious state, I heard one of the gendarmes say, "When that little Jew dies, just toss him onto the garbage heap and call the *Yeddishe Gemeinde* to pick him up and bury him."

The whipping had been administered powerfully. When I regained consciousness, I found myself in a jail cell, lying in a pool of my own blood. I was in pain, weak, and hot with fever. More than anything, I begged for water—and I drank. The sight of the torn, bleeding flesh on my back moved even the callous man on guard, who daily witnessed and participated in acts of human brutality. I must have been a pitiful sight to behold.

During the interrogation, I had mentioned that my uncle lived in Krosniewice. The guard contacted my uncle, Shaaye-Schloime, and allowed him to take me with him. I never learned what happened to the other man they had captured.

My uncle carried me to his house and placed me on a cot. He called a doctor, who also lived in the ghetto. After examining me, I overheard him saying, "If he lives through the night, he has a chance. He will need someone to stay with him to watch him and wash him with warm compresses. When his condition stabilizes, he will need a diet of orange juice and milk to help him recuperate." This was like asking for the moon.

In my delirium and moments of consciousness, I overheard my uncle's wife complaining about wasting good coal to keep my compresses warm. In times of distress, normally generous people sometimes become extremely selfish, even with their loved ones, in the battle for self-preservation. It was now winter in December 1940.

The Good Lord sent his healing angels. Yes, even human beings can turn into angels. News of my illness and needs spread throughout the ghetto. My good friend, Abram Danziger, organized my teenage friends into shifts to sit with me. They never left me without attention. During the next few days, my temperature normalized, and there was now hope for me to live.

Securing milk and orange juice for me was the next problem facing my uncle. One day, Mr. Chaim Arnavi came to my rescue. Even though he barely knew me, he believed in helping others, no matter the cost. Mr. Arnavi knew that to save a life is worth one's life savings. Using his money lavishly and sacrificially, Mr. Arnavi almost never failed to acquire milk and oranges for me on the black market.

With this nourishment and care, my strength slowly returned. My back was still black with clots of blood, and my body was still bruised. I thanked God that I was alive and slowly healing.

Trouble brings people together, sometimes even more so than happiness. During Mr. Arnavi's daily visits with me, our friendship grew. He repeatedly told me that he would always try to help me. I, in turn, overflowed in heartfelt appreciation for his generosity. "Dear God," I prayed, "help me and give me strength so that I may be able to repay this fine man's kindness and sacrifice for me." It would be quite some time before this prayer would be answered.

After three months, I was well again—or as well as could be expected. Mrs. Rose Issac gave a surprise party in honor of my recovery. With food bought on the black market, it was almost a feast.

When the party was over, I walked with a big, happy smile back to my uncle's house. To my dismay, I found the door bolted and the cot, which I had recuperated on, placed outside the door. My smile turned to tears. It seemed that my uncle and his family felt that they had done enough for me. Now that I was on my feet, I was on my own. Where to go? What to do?

Mrs. Issac's home was but a block away, and it was from there that I had come so happily. My face wet with tears, I knocked on her door. She opened the door, and I told her what had happened. Mrs. Issac embraced me and told me I had not one single worry. "My home is your home," she said. She led me to the hallway, pointed to a table against the wall, and showed me how easy it was to place bedding on it. I went to my uncle's home the following morning to pick up my few belongings and moved back into Mrs. Issac's two-room apartment.

The Issacs had a daughter, Zosia. Because I was well mannered and from a good family background, they dropped little hints such as, "Zosia is a fine girl. Isn't that so?" I took the hint. To please the Issacs, I took their daughter on strolls during the evening. I did this, not for love, but out of a feeling of obligation. Zosia was a fine girl, but she was no substitute for Ester, who had made my heart pulsate.

As I walked with Zosia, my relatives observed me. After a few days, they called me over, surrounded me and told me off. "How dare you be so thoughtless and selfish as to think about girls and celebrate while your parents are fighting for their lives and starving in Kutno!" Even though I was doing all I could for my family, tears came to my eyes, and I choked in speechlessness as I thought of my loving parents and sisters, helpless and far away.

A new edict soon broke the routine. The Krosniewice *Gemeinde* announced a quota of 100 men from our ghetto for temporary work elsewhere. Because I was a newcomer and young, I was among the first to be selected. They also placed Mr. Arnavi and Abram Danziger on the list, as well as my uncle's twin sons.

It was a sad day. I gathered my few articles of clothing, including my new shoes that my father had insisted I take along to face the unknown road ahead. Hurriedly, I said my good-byes and marched off to board the waiting train. We were all stunned to see the hundreds of armed soldiers who guarded the train and locked the cattle cars we were forced to board. After a full night's travel, we arrived in Hardt, near Poznan, and marched for miles to our first concentration camp.

Survival in the Camps

Looks can be deceiving, and I was certainly deceived. In front of us were newly built and freshly painted buildings that were to be our barracks. It was a joyous sight and I was elated at the thought that now, for the first time since the war began, I would be treated like a human being instead of a beast. I was somebody just like anyone else. No better and no worse. I felt important and this felt good.

Our new overlords directed us to a room containing twenty new bunk beds, each covered with two new blankets. Each bed also had a straw-filled pillow. In the center of the spacious room stood a brand spanking new potbellied stove for which we were given a very small ration of coal per night, exactly one bucketful of brickets. Each man had his own locker with a key, and it was the safest place to keep valuables. My eyes surveyed the room, and I jumped to an upper bunk and made it my own.

It turned out that my choice of an upper bunk was a wise one. I had privacy, and I avoided the frequent accident caused by the sick bladder of an upper bunk's occupant. Even more, I avoided the close inspection that the German officers frequently gave to the lower bunks, often not troubling themselves with the upper ones.

The German military worked like a machine. Without losing any time, they assembled us that evening and gave us a small cake of soap and a clean hand towel. We were given these instructions: (1) The property with which we were entrusted—blankets, towels, etc.—was to be carefully maintained. (2) If we lost or damaged any of them, we would be severely punished. (3) Our mission was now to work for the German military forces.

They engineered the camp routine to derive the most work for the smallest investment—simple housing and meager food. In essence, we were slaves of the German army, the *Wehrmacht*. Our daily routine was to wake up at 5:00 A.M., wash up by 5:20, breakfast at 5:30, clean up by 5:40, and line up at 6:00 for roll call.

The day had its full share of marching. We marched one block to the latrine, one block to the kitchen, and one hour to the work site. We marched in rain, shine, or storm.

The Nazis warned us against trying to avoid our work assignment. Goldbricking was strictly *verboten* (forbidden). They tied anyone claiming to be sick, with no detectable fever, to the "punishment pole," located in the center of the camp. The prisoners had to stay there, without food, toilet facilities, or shelter until nightfall. And there was no doctor in the camp's one first-aid station. During the following months, many died while tied to the punishment pole. Those poor prisoners obviously weren't feigning illness.

Our job was to construct a section of Hitler's *Autobahn*, a highway that eventually would link Berlin to Warsaw, and Warsaw to Moscow. Sixteen men constituted a work gang. Our foreman was Herr Philip Brandscheid, a German civilian. They gave us each a pick and a shovel to use on our road-building assignment. The Germans had surveyed, bulldozed, and cleared as much as their equipment could do. To us fell the task of handwork that was impractical for road-building machines. We constructed a miniature railroad by laying rails on cross ties after preparing and leveling the earth. We then pushed the rail carts, heavily laden with earth fill, to the road. The German taskmasters made full use of our hand labor.

On one occasion, the day's assignment was to dig a deep hole for a water tank. Watching sixteen undernourished bodies slave away at the backbreaking road work bored our foreman. Herr Brandscheid needed some sport—he craved sadistic fulfillment—and it was my turn to entertain him. Because I was only a little more than five feet tall, he purposely selected me to go into a hole that was over my head and shovel the dirt out. As hard as I tried to throw the dirt up so that others could shovel it away from the hole, I naturally failed. My foreman stood by and laughed with delight at my predicament. As I shoveled the dirt out, it would fall back and hit me on my head and face.

"Lazy Jew," he yelled, "why don't you stop being so lazy? You must work harder to get the job done!" After satisfying himself with this and other insults, Herr Brandscheid reached down and hit me on the head with his fast-swinging cane. My blood began to gush forth, and I saw stars.

I screamed out of fright and pain, and the *Baumeister*, or site supervisor, came running to see what had happened. When the supervisor saw the little figure of a man covered with blood, standing and screaming in the bottom of the deep pit, he demanded an explanation. Herr Brandscheid said that he was punishing me for my laziness.

The *Baumeister* thundered back at Brandscheid, "Why don't you put the big fellows in the pit and let him shovel the dirt away with the shorter ones?" He ordered the others to push me up out of the pit. The *Baumeister* took me to the nearby first-aid shack to have my wound washed and bandaged.

Within minutes, they marched—really dragged and carried—me back to my work area, then placed a shovel into my hands, and ordered me back to work again. Soon it was time for our half-hour break for lunch, which consisted of one piece of bread and a cup of black coffee. We looked forward to it, not only for the meager nourishment, but also because we had a few moments to breathe free.

It was now clear to me that the Nazis were using me as a tool—in more ways than one—and that my life was cheap. I finally understood that it was only what I could do for the Nazis that mattered. My survival depended on this new realization.

In truth, all men are created equal by the one Good Lord above. The fortunes and misfortunes of men, however, certainly differ. For the first few days at Camp Hardt, I had visions of being on a faraway isle sharing common joys and common troubles. My bed was like everyone else's, and my meager watery soup which was called food was no better and no worse than anyone else's. This gave me a false feeling of equality and security.

It turned out not to be so. Nearly all of my fellow prisoners had relatives on the outside. In some places, the war had not yet uprooted everyone's lives. Many prisoners wrote home complaining of poor treatment and inadequate food, and their relatives sent them packages of food, clothing, soap, and other personal items. My neighbors also received letters of love and sympathy to encourage them. My situation was the reverse. My parents and sisters were still suffering in the Kutno Ghetto. They needed my comfort and help. I carried this extra burden.

What could I do? I could not mail my parents and sisters food or clothing, but I could at least relieve their anxiety over my welfare. My letters to them were always cheerful, and I would tell them how wonderful things were for me at Camp Hardt. My "white" lies served a good purpose and cost me nothing. I became a good fiction writer.

My father happily and boastfully wrote to the father of a fellow Camp Hardt prisoner. My neighbor's father had received letters of woe from his son. They could not understand the contradictory nature of our reports of conditions at the same camp.

Even in this dismal setting, there was a ray of friendship and help for me. My friend from Krosniewice, Chaim Arnavi, who had earlier saved my life by obtaining the necessary orange juice and milk for my recovery, was in the camp with me. These conditions of shortages and deprivations would generally force many to think solely of themselves, but Mr. Arnavi rose above the ordinary. He shared his packages of food, mostly bread, that he received from his family in Krosniewice. My thanks knew no bounds. A slice of bread to a hungry man is priceless, and, like everyone else, I was always hungry.

What could I do in return for such great favors? I felt that I had to show my appreciation in some way. I planned to wash his clothes, clean his shoes, and darn his socks, but Mr. Arnavi refused to be catered to or rewarded for his kindness. I begged and finally insisted. Moreover, I threatened that if he would not let me do something for him, I would not let him do anything for me. He finally gave in.

So I washed his clothes and mine, too. What had started out to be white clothes had darkened into gray or almost black. Like everyone else, I had to wash without soap. We lived and worked hard under filthy conditions. Our previously white undergarments were now dark, but at least they were as clean as possible. We still took pride in trying to keep clean.

We worked hard and long hours. They gave us only one loaf of bread to divide among five men each day. This was less than enough to keep body and soul together. We were always hungry. We did not dream of women, sex, or money. We dreamed only of that rainbow in the sky—a loaf of bread to eat. If only we had one full loaf of bread of our own to eat. . . . If only we did not have to share the one loaf among five. . . .

We devised a plan to do just that. Each day our crew chief divided our one loaf into five pieces. We, in turn, cut each piece in half. We ate one half and stored the other half, accumulating it for the next five days. At the end of the five-day span, we drew lots to determine who would receive the first full loaf for his own use. The others would have to use their saved-up bread until their turn came to receive a full loaf to eat. The thought that we would finally get one full loaf of bread for our own feast was worth all the waiting and saving.

My turn was third, and I eagerly looked forward to the banquet that was soon to be mine. To be fair and avoid arguments, all the crew chiefs drew lots for the available loaves. While they all had approximately the same weight, some looked larger than the others. "Dear God," I prayed, "let my crew chief draw loaf 'G' so he can turn it over to me." Bread loaf "G" looked the largest. My prayer was answered. He picked up the largest loaf and gave it to me. My joy was indescribable. I felt that my troubles were over, at least for a few days.

Hungry and salivating though I was, I had trained myself to think and save and plan for tomorrow. I controlled my strong desire to bite even a small part of my loaf of bread. What a joy it was to know that a full loaf of bread was waiting for me— and me alone—to eat and enjoy on the morrow. I locked my treasured prize in my locker with my stored-up bread. I went to sleep happy and secure, knowing that I was rich and had enough to eat.

The next morning after I washed, I opened my locker just to fondle and hug my loaf of bread, thanking God for bringing it forth from the earth. I looked. I looked again. I checked to see if I had opened the right locker with my key, although each key supposedly fit only one locker. I was speechless and bewildered. My whole world collapsed. All my bread was stolen, and I was now more hungry than ever.

Not only that, what could I eat for the next few days? Nothing.

In my despair, I ran hither and yon. "Please give me back my bread!" I cried to the other men in my barracks. "Have you seen my loaf of bread? Don't be so cruel. Give me back my bread." The only response I received was silence. "Please," I said to the German officer in charge, "help me with a little bread," and I told him the whole story. He listened with half an ear and told me to get back to work, that there was nothing he could do for me. Who, I thought, but God could help me now?

Mr. Arnavi was again the Lord's angel. The story of my stolen loaf had spread. Mr. Arnavi came to me and said, "Don't worry. I will share my bread with you." So it was. His word was better than gold.

Life at Camp Hardt was never without tension. They had warned us about our responsibility for the blankets, straw pillows, and other items entrusted to us. To lose ordinary German property could mean a day tied to the punishment pole without food and toilet facilities, or a whipping, or even death. My cousin, Jacob, who was more than a year younger but nearly one foot taller than I, came to me one morning with a look of calamity on his face. He could hardly speak coherently. I calmed him, and he told me that someone had stolen one of his blankets. He was shaking with fright.

"What am I to do now?" he lamented. I saw the deep despair and fear in his eyes. Quickly I pulled one of the two blankets from my own bed and gave it to him. I made him swear not to breathe a word to anyone. He ran out dazed, but thankful.

I thought quickly. After we began marching to the roll

call area, I ran back as though I had forgotten something. There was no one in the room. Quickly, I eased the first blanket that I could reach, tore it off the bed, and placed it on my own bed. Out I ran and lined up with the others, and off to work we went.

Miracle of miracles! When we all returned to our quarters that evening, everybody—but everybody—had two blankets! Perhaps everyone had the same solution that I did. It would have been wonderful to have had three blankets under which to keep warm, but not at the expense of another. We were all freezing, as before.

The demands and pressures at Camp Hardt emotionally affected my cousin, Jacob. The anxiety he had experienced over his stolen blanket was too much for him. At the line-up the next morning, there was one person missing—Jacob. Even though the Germans sounded the sirens and searched extensively, Jacob was nowhere to be found.

When we arrived at our *Baustelle*, or work site, we were surprised to see the figure of a man wrapped in a blanket sitting there. It was Jacob. Intensive questioning by the Germans revealed that Jacob had awakened during the night. He had imagined that he had overslept and that everyone else was already at work. Fearful of being punished, he wrapped himself in his blanket to protect it from thieves. As the guard at the gate slept, Jacob quietly walked by and onto the work site, where he sat dazed until morning. Even the Germans could clearly see that he had lost his mind and was not faking. They made him a water boy until he recovered.

Things were to get worse and not better. In November 1941, the freezing rains and snow came. We marched and worked as usual. Neither mud, rain, snow, nor ice, nor howling, freezing winds kept us from our tasks. Our shoes and clothes were soaking wet and could not dry out overnight. The next morning, we had to put on the same wet, cold clothes again. We shivered in the freezing cold, but the routine was the same. We marched. We worked. We hungered. We dropped off to sleep for a few hours, until morning brought on the same punishment again.[1]

My shoes, like our minds and bodies, were disintegrating. I had been wearing my old shoes, while saving the new pair my father had given me. The Germans heard my plea for new shoes and did not know I had a spare pair. Without shoes, I could not walk or work, so they gave me a pair of shoes. They were the wrong size and had wooden soles, but they were shoes, and I wore them. I considered myself lucky to have a new pair of shoes. They were higher than my old ones, and warmer.

Within hours, my happiness turned to gloom. Snow and ice began attacking the wooden soles as I marched to work, and I felt as though I were walking on uneven stilts. I had to stop often to scrape off the snow with my hands and then run ahead to take my place in line. I was always running.

Winter came. Our hands and bodies were frozen and numb, with no protection from the cold. We worked as before, able to keep warm only by working the shovel and moving around. The simple task of urinating or defecating became a major problem. Our frozen fingers could not bend to unbutton our pants or handle our organs. In the outhouse, we would privately struggle for only a moment or two before Herr Brandscheid would bang on the door with his cane and shout, "*Heraus du Hund!*" or, "Get out here, you dog!" He would give us permission to go to the outhouse, but we had to return without even beginning to relieve ourselves. We twisted and cramped with pain, but returned to work for fear of being tied to the punishment pole, or beaten to death. Perhaps, by a miracle, we could get permission again to go to the outhouse and would be more successful.[2]

As hard as it was to stay warm during the day, it was even harder at night. Trying to sleep at night in our freezing quar-

1. Abe spent most of 1941 in the concentration camp at Hardt. Having invaded the Soviet Union on June 22, 1941, the Nazis were outside Moscow, Russia's capitol, by the time the November freezing rains and snows began. Throughout the Nazi trek across Russian territory, Nazi murder squads, called *Einsatzgruppen*, murdered up to 2 million Soviet Jews. At Auschwitz, during the month of September 1941, Soviet prisoners of war were used in the testing of Zyclon B, the gas pellets used for mass extermination in gas chambers.

2. While Abe was struggling to stay alive in the freezing ice and snow of the Polish winter, the United States had entered the war following Japan's attack on Pearl Harbor on December 7, 1941, and Germany's declaration of war on the United States on December 11.

ters was nearly impossible. Our ration of one pail of coal each night was like a drop in the ocean. After an hour, we were cold again. We went to bed each night fearing that we would freeze to death before dawn, as so many prisoners did. We had to find a way to keep warm in the night. We put our heads together to find a remedy.

At the opposite end of the camp, the Germans stored their supply of coal. If we could get some, we would be a little better off, but how? It was a question of survival. The twenty men who lived in our room studied the problem carefully. The searchlight on the tower made a slow sweep of the camp throughout the night. It took eight minutes. Our only hope was to run behind the light with an empty pail, hoping to make it back with some coal before the light made its circle. To be caught would mean certain death by hanging, but not to get the coal meant certainly to freeze to death. Each man in our barracks had to take his chances until he could bring back three pails full of coal, which we placed in a box. We survived at the risk of our lives.

We also took turns accepting the responsibility of keeping the fire going, and the heat from our red-hot potbellied stove was not wasted. Our hungry, searching eyes discovered potato peels that were thrown out behind the kitchen. We assigned a different man each night to risk his life and bring back some potato peels. We washed them and placed them on top of the stove. These browned potato peels weren't quite like modern-day potato chips, but for our starving tummies, these were royal delicacies.

Life was an unending routine of hard labor that some tried in vain to escape. To make the most of their Jewish slaves, the German Command ran the camp with precision. One Monday morning, as Christmas loomed ahead, the Germans' precision count discovered five men missing. Sirens sounded, hounds barked, and whistles screeched while Germans ran to and fro, but nowhere could the five men be found.

I could almost taste the frustration and self-blame that our German overlords felt. How could five lowly Jews elude the Master Race and escape from such a secure, well-guarded camp? Their escape clearly pained and insulted the Germans. It was a question of honor. How dare a Jew dishonor a German!

For nearly four days, the hunt went on. Around the clock the Nazis sought the escapees, relentlessly, thoroughly. They pressed every available German into service. The five Jews had to be found.

On Thursday afternoon, as we returned from our day's work, our overlords whistled for joy and greeted us with superior smiles. In answer to our curious glances and questions, the Nazis proudly informed us that they had caught the escapees and had thrown them into jail. You would have thought they had found a million dollars.

On Sunday morning, we were informed that we would be fed a festive meal for lunch—a fatty soup with floating pieces of raisin bread. The Germans were celebrating—but what? As Christmas was nearing and they were away from home, the Germans needed some diversion, some entertainment, some fun. They had finally caught the escapees. These five Jews were to supply the recreation.

The Nazis loved to hang prisoners for entertainment, while at the same time frightening the other prisoners. They forced a detail of Jews to build a gallows for five. It was as perfect and splendorous as possible under the circumstances. The commandant ordered us all to encircle and face the gallows. The German guards watched us carefully to be sure that we did not take our eyes off the condemned prisoners. All the Nazis were present in their best uniforms. Even about ten women, also in Nazi uniforms, were there to watch the spectacle. We had to stand at attention while they led the condemned Jews at gunpoint to the gallows.

Three of the prisoners had steeled themselves. They saw the end as a sad but inevitable event that they could not control. They kept their dignity without even a whimper, as though they had mastered the Master Race. The other two cried and begged for mercy, but their pleas went unanswered. When they knew they had but seconds to live, they begged their assembled friends to inform their families of their deaths. As they were shouting their last pleas, the scaffold fell and the men were hanged until dead.

The Nazis ate up the show, as though they had won the war.[3] We were ordered to remain at attention for the next hour as the men dangled dead. Our feet became numb from the cold and the motionless standing, while the Nazis rubbed their hands and tapped their feet. Finally, they took the bodies down. The German officers were satisfied that the men were indeed dead, that we had learned a frightful lesson, and that they had had their pre-Christmas entertainment; then they ordered us to leave.

Our hearts were sad and heavy as we returned to our barracks. What could we say? What could we do? The Germans had made slaves of us and were using us for sport. Every one of us, almost at the same moment, turned his eyes and mouth upward to God in prayer. As though someone were leading us, we all joined in saying "Kaddish," a prayer for those five of us who died for freedom but won only death. There was a hush as we reflected on life, on God, on our families. We went to sleep, or tried to.

Darkness fell. Our stomachs could not accept food. The Germans never did offer us our evening meal that day.

On Monday morning, we expected permission for a few minutes to give these men a funeral, even though our work crew had never had an occasion to know these men or speak to them. We had already designated one of us to recite the prayers. The Germans, however, did not consider them human and allowed no funeral. We never found out exactly what happened to their bodies, but we know the Nazis treated them as garbage.[4]

The next day, the Nazis assigned us the usual day's work. They assigned our work crew to Herr Roter. As his name implied, he had a reddish face. Herr Roter commanded us to push sand carts on narrow rails, from the sand piles to the work site. There we had to dump the sand onto a wooden platform that Herr Roter had nicknamed *"der Hund."* It was back-

3. In fact, because of the harsh Russian winter, the war against the Soviet Union was beginning to turn against the Nazis when they were unable to take Moscow by the end of December.

4. Mass killings begin at Chelmno death camp on December 8, 1941, using specially built mobile vans to gas (with engine exhaust) Jews and Gypsies. In January 1942, 10,000 Jews were deported from the Lodz Ghetto to Chelmno.

breaking work. We had to keep the carts upright and balanced, so as not to tilt them over and spill the sand. Woe and lashes at the punishment pole would have greeted us for spilling the sand. We worked rapidly and hard for hours. If we slowed down a bit, Herr Roter would call us by his favorite phrase, "*Du verdamter Hund!* (You damn dog!)" This warning carried the threat of a whack or two. Herr Roter conveniently carried a crowbar for this purpose, and, of course, as the tool he needed for moving the rails.

Even an innocent mistake brought severe punishment. After working a while, Herr Roter shouted at me to bring him "*der Hund.*" Having just heard Herr Roter disgrace my friend, David, by calling him "*der Hund*," I naturally fetched David. "*Nein. Nein. Verdamter Hund!*" he shouted as he pointed to the wooden platform, which he also called "*der Hund.*" *Hund* was his favorite word, and I had brought him the wrong *Hund*. Even Herr Roter laughed, but this was the only second of amusement I was to know. A moment later, Herr Roter's true character reasserted itself. He had to punish me, even for this simple and innocent error. He made me carry more than half the tools used by our crew back to the storage shed, near our barracks. The others carried less than their normal load.

Another week passed. One day they called my name for mail. I had never received mail before. Who on God's earth could or would be able to write to me? I wondered. To my delight, they handed me a package. I excitedly opened it and saw crusty, golden bread, a jar of thick soup, and shiny cookies. It was like a box of jewels to me. "Perhaps it is a miracle," I thought as I lifted the bread.

Then I found the enclosed letter, which read: "Dear Abe, please give this parcel to your cousin, Mendel. He can receive only one package per month, and we felt you would not mind us using your name to help your cousin." Mendel's mother had sent this package from Krosniewice. Hungry and tempted though I was, my home and religious training had taught me never to steal from or deceive another. Taking my free time to deliver the package—it being Sunday, our day off—a happy thought came to me: Surely my fine cousin, Mendel, will reward me by sharing part of his bread and cookies!

I walked in to find Mendel bowing and shaking to and fro, in the customary Jewish manner, as he mumbled his prayers. With a show of false piety, he motioned for me to leave him alone; it is a sin to interrupt a conversation with God for the sake of speaking to a man. Mendel glanced my way again, however, and saw the package. He quickly ceased praying and ran to grab it. Even as he was opening it, he began telling me that he had received a letter about the package and a list of its contents. In the same breath, he accused me of stealing much of what had been sent and demanded that I give it back to him. He was a shrewd, selfish, mean, and hypocritical man. Mendel accused me unjustly to deprive me of a few cookies and a few crumbs of bread. Mendel was a praying man, but evidently he was not one who took his prayers seriously. The ritual, yes, but the meaning of the Jewish teachings, no.

It was now winter, early in 1942.[5] We returned to Camp Hardt after a day of toil to learn that some of us would be transferred to another camp. I received this news with mixed emotions. My mind overflowed with questions. Now what? Will I be chosen? Where will I be sent? Is it my turn to die?

After our regular meal, light as it was, we lined up nervously in the middle of the camp to hear the news of our future. A Nazi SS officer called out names from a list. My cousin, Jacob, and I were on the list, along with Abram Danziger. We had to assemble at another spot, along with about fifty others. The weather was cold, and the ground was frozen with snow. My garments were showing signs of long wear; they were hardly better than no garments at all.

I looked around at the faces of the others gathered to leave. I noticed that my friend, Mr. Arnavi, was missing. It saddened me to realize that he was not coming with us. Looking at the ground, feeling the cold air, and missing my friend, my body began

5. On January 20, 1942, in the Berlin suburb Wannsee, fourteen top Nazi officials, invited by Reinhard Heydrich, met to develop plans for the total destruction of the Jews, the "Final Solution." Information gathered from the *Einsatzgruppen* (killing units), from the special mobile vans for gassing (at Chelmno), and from Zyclon B testing (at Auschwitz) was used to organize a plan that entailed mass extermination in industrial-size gas chambers and crematoria.

to shiver with the cold fear of uncertainty. "This means that I shall have to make new friends at our new destination," I thought. "God, I hope I can make it." We went back to our barracks to rest for the night.

The next morning, after a very light breakfast, we prepared for our journey. I put my few belongings into my rucksack, including the pair of shoes that my dear father had reminded me to carry. I joined the others at the gate, where we boarded the trucks that were already waiting for us. We were loaded to capacity, with no room to spare. The Nazis drove us to the railroad station, and we boarded the waiting rail cars, cattle style. Our train ride lasted about eight hours. Food was nonexistent. Our bodies suffered from hunger and exposure.

When the train finally stopped, we marched for about an hour to our new destination, Gross-Rosen Concentration Camp, near Breslau, Poland. Even though we marched through one foot of snow, I kept my good pair of shoes tied around my neck. I wanted to save them until I really needed them.

Two SS guards approached us as we passed through the camp gate. They divided us into two lines, so that one of them could talk to each person. In checking us over, the guard told me to put my rucksack down. Noticing my new shoes, he told me, with concern in his voice, "You better take your shoes with you. You will not get any of your belongings back."

I took his advice and put the new shoes under my belt. He was a middle-aged man who felt somewhat sorry for my condition after noticing that I was wearing worn-out wooden-soled shoes. His small gesture would soon prove to save my life.

Next we went to the camp washroom where we stripped for a delousing shower, after which we put our old clothes back on. They assigned us to our barracks. We didn't know whether they had sent us here to live or to die.

We heard a whistle blow and shouts of "*schnell*" (fast), as the Nazis ordered us to line up. My eyes beheld an unbelievable sight. Men were running around barefoot in the snow, as though they were going out of their minds. With emaciated bodies, they did not look like human beings anymore. My thoughts went far afield. What has happened to these people? What will happen to me?

Why did they send me here, and how did I get into this position?

To keep us in line, the Nazi SS guards whipped us like cattle. When we lined up for our supper—it could hardly have been called supper—they permitted one man at a time to go forward in the line and receive his portion of bread. The guard then whipped the next person, which was his signal to go forward and receive his ration of bread. This whipping deeply hurt our exhausted, frozen bodies. Would this small morsel of bread have to do me from now on? Who knows when I will get my next meal?

While walking back to the barracks in the snow, with bread in hand, my mind wandered back to Camp Hardt. My God, that camp was like heaven compared to this camp. This camp was hell; that much I knew. Upon entering the barracks, my supposed new home, I saw that there were no provisions for heating this cold, dreary building.

No human being could have remained healthy under the conditions existing in this camp and in others like it. Our bladders were weak and not functioning properly. As a result, we found ourselves needing to go to the latrine many times during the night. Four times, five times, and sometimes more, we had to trek through the snow to urinate, as there were no toilet facilities in the barracks. Our only course of action was to use the latrine facilities, a block away, to get relief. I thought that if this was how I must live, then I would learn to survive.[6]

Like animals, we become cunning when faced with hardships. We found two large bowls in the building. We used them to pass our water and get relief, without making the long walk through the snow to the latrine. When these bowls filled, one of us had to empty the contents on the snow outside the barracks. We staked our lives against the possibility of being caught.

To our great sorrow, we soon learned that we would have to eat out of these same bowls. We cleaned the bowls as best we

6. One might wonder how such conditions could be allowed to exist in a concentration camp. Was there no protest from international agencies? The Nazis had thought of this possibility, and to insure secrecy, on November 24, 1941, they began construction of a "model" camp called Theresienstadt. This camp was used to show groups like the International Red Cross and the Vatican what life in the camps was like. Theresienstadt, almost nothing like the other camps, was designed to keep prying eyes away from what the Nazis were really doing to Jews in the camps and in the ghettos.

could with just the snow outside our building. My God, how any of us survived is beyond my comprehension. Six men to eat their food from one bowl. Animals had it better.

The next morning, two of us took the bowls and lined up to receive whatever food was available for our barracks. They gave us some rutabaga soup to carry back. This was to be our nourishment for all day! I could not believe what was happening to me. Walking with this bowl of soup back to the barracks, I thought, "My Dear God, how can six starving people eat at one time from this bowl?"

These people being very hungry, cold, and run down, I thought my life would be in danger, like an animal, to bring this meager ration for six men to eat. I entered the barracks and put the bowl on the table. Sure enough, I saw the men grab for this ration like animals. I shall never forget this most unbearable sight of human beings, including myself, gulping food for survival. "If there be a God," I wondered, "where is He now?"

When we finished eating, we took the bowls to the washroom and cleaned them as well as we could. Then we returned to the barracks and lay there on the bunks for several hours, awaiting our fate.

The soup we were served at Gross-Rosen was extremely salty and was distributed in large, metal milk containers.[7] When filled with the extremely salty mixture, each container weighed well over 100 pounds. The Germans selected different prisoners each day for the deadly task of carrying these containers to the barracks. They were difficult for healthy men to carry; the sick prisoners could scarcely muster the strength to carry them at all. If they didn't die trying to carry the heavy containers, the Nazis would often murder them for not obeying orders.

One day they assigned this dangerous task to a Greek Jew. As weak as he was, he understood the danger to his life. Using almost faultless German, he replied twice to the SS officer that he could not do it. The Nazi's ego could not accept a Jew's

7. The commander of the Gross-Rosen SS killed more than 65,000 Russian inmates in six months by feeding them soup made of grass, water, and quantities of salt, followed by quantities of cold water. "They contracted dysentery and died like flies." Konnilyn Feig, *Hitler's Death Camps* (New York: Holmes and Meier, 1979), p. 206.

refusal to obey a direct order. He clubbed the Greek Jew, and blood streamed from his head.

Undaunted, the Jew yelled, "I know you can kill me, but don't ever forget what is waiting for you when the war is over. You know what I am talking about!" These words must have struck a fearful chord in this SS officer. For whatever reason, he stopped clubbing the prisoner and slowly walked away. The Greek Jew gasped in relief and slowly recovered from his wounds.

The next day, the Nazi guards suddenly ordered us to board trucks for departure. Without any time for preparation, we boarded the waiting trucks and began our journey to Bolkenheim, a Gross-Rosen subcamp. At least we didn't have to walk.

Although Hungarian Jews were in leadership positions at Bolkenheim, we suffered miserably at their hands. They treated us as harshly as the Nazis did, pushing us and beating us and constantly reminding us that our existence was meaningless.

Two Hungarian Jews led several of us to the camp infirmary for our first work assignment. About twelve prisoners were moaning in pain on their beds, suffering from various ailments. Disease was rampant at Bolkenheim. It was a miracle to live through the horrible conditions there, as in most camps, without being stricken with some life-threatening disease. The German medics made no attempt to cure the sick prisoners. In front of us, within minutes, some breathed their last. As two of us strained to carry the corpses to their burial place, we could still feel warmth in some of the bodies. They were not fully dead, but we could do nothing about it. The other men on our detail struggled to dig large mass graves in the hard, frozen earth. We threw the bodies into the pit and returned to repeat the routine.

At the end of this horrible day, we were trucked back to Gross-Rosen.

The camp doctors soon examined us in the barracks next to ours. After passing the exam, the doctor told me that I would be one of those lucky ones to be transferred to another camp. He told me that, as a laborer, I would be treated as a human being. Some form of happiness must have shown on my face. My day was approaching, and I soon would be free of this hell on earth.

In the morning, I excitedly anticipated leaving this camp, only to have my happiness shattered. The camp guards ordered me to go to a farm near the camp, to clear the grounds of snow. The farmer who oversaw our efforts kept us moving with a big club. He continually beat our backs and ordered us to work faster, faster, faster, harder, harder, harder. I thought many times that I would drop. I was weak. I was cold. I was hungry. I had to go forward or be beaten to death.

I still do not know how or why I was helped to stay alive during these most trying times. There were times I felt that death would be happiness—but I kept working because I was afraid not to.

In the evening we trekked our way back to the camp, completely exhausted and hungry. Our spirits were below rock bottom. When we went to our barracks—the coldest-looking place I had ever seen—we just collapsed. After resting a while, we sat up and talked to each other. We discussed what we had done that day, what we thought about our existence, and *if* and *when* we would ever be transferred out of this camp.

After a short time, I noticed that a friend of mine, Rabinowicz, was missing. He had worked with me all day, and he must have felt the same as I felt—hopelessly exhausted. I wondered where he was.

Soon he entered the barracks with happiness in his eyes, and he called me aside. He said he was leaving very soon on a transport. He was sorry that I was to stay in this camp. Indeed this concerned me greatly. He had just bribed a guard through a contact, and the guard had placed him on the list to go. I asked Rabinowicz what I could do to get placed on this list—to get out of this hellhole. He told me that I needed something for a bribe. He had used tobacco.

I stopped for a minute and thought. I felt my body and searched my mind for something to use as a bribe. My thoughts were soon answered—my new shoes that my father insisted I take with me might now save my life. Thank God I had been allowed to keep them when I entered this camp.

"I have a pair of new shoes," I told Rabinowicz. "They're made of real leather. Could they be used as a bribe?"

"I'll try," Rabinowicz said and he ran out. In no time at all he returned. "Abe, give me the shoes," he exclaimed. He made his contact, and my name was placed on the list to finally leave this dreaded camp. I had to get ready and go outside immediately, as they were already calling out the names. I ran outside, heard my name called, and got in line. I was ecstatic about leaving this God-forsaken place.

The thought of leaving also brought sadness. My cousin, Jacob, who had earlier suffered a mental collapse over his missing blanket at Camp Hardt, was now functioning almost normally in this camp. He had a choice job, working in the kitchen. Being next to food was like being next to heaven. Jacob ran to my side when he learned that I was on the transfer list. With tears falling from his eyes, he begged me to do something to remain there, where he could help me with food and other comforts.

Nothing, even the assurance of a full belly of food and other comforts, could entice me to stay. I had visions of going mad myself if I remained in a setting where so many people walked around half-dazed, showing signs of mental collapse.

Working to Live

Being an honored worker on this particular day had more than its typical share of good points. They fed us generously and gave us some bread for the journey. They didn't tell us where we were going or how long we would travel, but I was happy to have something in my stomach and to be on my way out of this place. At the gate, our group of about 100 men boarded the waiting trucks and began our journey to the railroad station.

Upon our arrival, we could hardly believe our eyes. There, before us, stood civilized, comfortable passenger cars—not the cattle cars or freight cars we had expected. They had soft seats and we sat like human beings. We had almost forgotten that the world outside was inhabited by humans and run for humans. I looked around in disbelief—but it was true. We were sitting in comfortable seats as though we really mattered. Soon, the train slowly pulled out of the station, and we were rolling into the night toward another camp.

When the sun rose, we could see a city, and the train soon came to a halt in Berlin. Waiting trucks hauled us to Camp Dretz, not far from the city.

Again, we were treated like humans, and it was good. There were no guards at the entrance to the camp. We were guided into a room where warm showers with soap and towels waited for us. Following this, as always, we were deloused. This time, however, small air pressure spray guns with diluted disinfectant were waiting for us to use personally and privately. We felt important and dignified. It was also good to know that if any lice clung to our bodies they would be fumigated. I recalled, by contrast, the dozens of other times we were taken like pieces of material and dumped into disinfectant tanks. It felt good to have our self-respect again.

They then called us to assembly. The spokesman was also a Jewish prisoner of war, Mr. Abbe (pronounced in German *Ahbey*). "We will not treat you as prisoners," he said, according to the instructions he had received from German authorities, "but as foreign workers. You will be treated well here. All that we require of you is that you work hard. I think you will find the facilities satisfactory." He pointed to a four-foot row of fencing and said, "On the other side of that fence is a contingent of French prisoners of war; behind them is a group of Russian prisoners. You are all here to work. You will now have something to eat, and then you will be shown your barracks. That is all."

Another pleasant surprise awaited us. After our orientation, they led us into a large, well-lit, almost luxurious room. It took us some time to realize that we were in a large dining hall. Very few of us had ever seen such a sight because most of the prisoners had always eaten at home, and we had little experience with large-city dining. We were invited to take our seats around rectangular tables that seated about six each. This was to be surpassed by an even more pleasant surprise. A French waiter walked up to our table and asked for our individual choice of food. Not only that, but after we ordered the food, they actually brought it to us! Imagine that . . . we were sitting like paying customers in an exclusive restaurant and waited on by French personnel (also war prisoners).

The atmosphere was more than conducive to eating well. We were so hungry that we needed no atmosphere really, but it helped and we appreciated it. After we finished our food, they asked whether we wanted more—and we all wanted more and more. The aroma of various delicious foods mingled in the air, and we thought we were little kings and princes. The atmosphere was as luxurious as the food was tasty. We all came alive. We seemed to see better, hear better, walk better, smile better, digest better. We threw out our chests with pride and stood up tall. It was a very new experience for all of us.

Unfortunately, we were never to get a repeat of this luxurious experience. Evidently, through someone's error, they had allowed us into the canteen reserved for foreign workers, with the exception of Russians and Jews. The food we received in our own barracks, however, was wholesome and tasty. Even though we were not waited on or offered seconds and thirds, we found ourselves happily fed and well treated, in comparison to the other camps.[1]

The Germans allowed us several days of vacation from work as a rejuvenation period. They fattened us up, not for the kill, but for the will to work. They had cut the camp out of a park or forest. The weather was cool but mild, and we walked around and gazed at the beautiful trees that were everywhere around us. Across the wire, I used my knowledge of the German language to communicate with several Frenchmen whose quarters adjoined ours. Slightly better treated, they were sympathetic and helpful, giving us extra food and encouraging words.

Our French neighbors told us that the Germans would feed us and keep us alive only if we worked productively and earned our keep. Otherwise, our lives were cheap, and they would send us to the Warsaw Ghetto to be killed.

Soon, Mr. Abbe called our Jewish sector of approximately 100 men to line up for selection by various craftsmen. First came a well-dressed civilian, who courteously asked for forty construction workers. I, like almost everyone else, raised my hand to volunteer. They did not select me, as my small frame did not show that I could be a robust construction worker. They selected the huge builds of men who could obviously handle heavy work with ease. Next came a German civilian who requested painters. I did not volunteer, feeling that my lack of experience as a painter might displease my new employer. The last request was for four electricians. My mind began racing. I figured that the Germans would never allow a Jew to do the important, technical electrical work. What they probably needed was an

1. It was the spring of 1942 for Abe, and plans made at the Wannsee Conference in January were now underway. In east Poland, gas chambers at Sobibor and Belzec began operation in March 1942; on June 1, 1942, Treblinka would begin operation. During the summer and fall of 1942, Jews both in Germany and in Poland would be deported to these killing facilities.

electrician's helper. As a young boy in Poland, I often assisted my neighbor, Mr. Pytelewsky, with his electrical work. I always enjoyed it and understood much of what I did, and he always praised me for my helpfulness.

Quickly I raised my hand and eagerly volunteered. Here was a job that I could do—and better do if I wanted to be numbered among the living. Four men volunteered, and Mr. Abbe told us that a German civilian would come to pick us up the next day. About twelve men were still without work. They had reason for concern about their status. I felt secure in the knowledge that I had been chosen.

The next morning, however, brought me an unexpected disappointment. Mr. Abbe called out, "Where are the four electricians? Someone has come to pick you up for work." As if out of nowhere, five men stepped out. The fifth man, who had not stepped forward the previous day, was Aaron Glickman, one of my close friends. He had become fearful for his life when he was not given a work assignment.

It was a sudden confrontation for which I was not prepared. I was signaled to stay behind. I explained to Mr. Abbe that I was one of the four selected the day before. Mr. Abbe, who had learned to be callous and unfeeling, shrugged it off and said, "This is not my choice. The decision rests with the German civilian who pushed you aside. There is nothing I can do."

It required a special personality and mentality to be a German underling. Yes, it was good to be in a position of authority—to be a boss, to live a little better, and to eat a little better—but one's heart had to be made of stone. One had to throw his feeling and compassion away. I never aspired to lick the boots of the Germans in ordering others around. I did not have the heart to survive at the cost of someone else's sorrow and misery.

It was a sad moment for me to contemplate the future without a work assignment. There were no other requests for workers. The request for electricians was the last. Camp Dretz was for workers only, and I worried about what was to happen to me.

To make my wounds saltier, the workmen returned from their assignments and told wonderful stories about how well they were treated. The construction workers were fed delicacies and were given cigarettes and food to take home, but they did have to work hard. The others had similar tales to accompany the smiles of satisfaction on their faces. Each man had his picture taken for purposes of identification, allowing them entry into the camouflaged, underground ammunition factory where they worked. Finally, the electrical workers (with whom I was to work) tore my heart out when they boasted of very good food, fine treatment, and very little work. Aaron Glickman, who had stolen my job, boasted the loudest.

For two nights, I tossed and turned with worry. During the day I looked around at the dozen or so men not selected for work. They all appeared sick and weak. I knew in my heart that their end was annihilation, and I worried about dying with them.

Two days later, the morning sun shone a miracle. About ten o'clock that morning, a German civilian, Herr Krämer, asked Mr. Abbe for two electrician's helpers. They chose Glickman and me. Glickman had finished his other assignment.

As I looked around, I could see that among those left without a work assignment—and therefore doomed—was Mrs. Rose Issac's son, Eizik. My mind recalled how, in Krosniewice, he had begrudged me the luxury of sleeping on four chairs in his parents' home. He reasoned that they could rent this space to another, while I had no means of payment. Now it was his turn to be on the receiving end and to receive no mercy, no heart, no consideration. There was justice and retribution in God's hands, I thought.

Revenge was sweet, but not for long. Sadly, I learned that he and six others were sent to Warsaw, where they met death.[2]

Herr Krämer was a German civilian in charge of overall operations of the Bergman Elektrizät Werks. The task of the BEW was to electrify various underground ammunition factories. Herr Krämer was a fine gentleman, but was under much pressure. He had a difficult assignment in reaching his goals without undue delay. Herr Krämer kept his conversations with us to a minimum,

2. The deportation of Warsaw Ghetto Jews to Treblinka began on July 22, 1942. On July 28 the Underground Jewish Fighting Organization formed in the Warsaw Ghetto.

pertaining only to the job at hand, with never any small talk. He was a man with pride and noble carriage.

My camp mate, Aaron Glickman, hailed from the big city of Warsaw, Poland, and he never let anyone forget it. (He had much less to be proud of than the humblest Texan.) They assigned Glickman as an electrician's helper to Leo Blum, a master craftsman.

It was my good fortune to be assigned as helper to another master craftsman, Herr Heinrich Sträter. We referred to him as "Herr Meister." Compared to my life in the ghettos and camps, working with Herr Sträter was like night and day. I had been degraded and treated worse than an animal for so long, but now my boss talked to me like a human being. My first day working for Herr Sträter was almost like working for my own father. He even boosted my sagging morale by telling me that, after all, he was no better than I.

Herr Sträter put my mind at ease by assuring me that, as long as I worked for him, I would never need to worry about going hungry. My boss kept his promise and brought me delicious lunch in overflowing quantity. In addition, he gave me extra sandwiches to take home. It was like manna from heaven.

After finishing my first meal, he marveled that I had eaten such a large quantity of food. "How can you eat so much?" he asked. "I am a much larger man, and I can't eat that much myself."

"Only a starving man," I explained respectfully, "could know and appreciate hunger and the need for food. It was a delicious meal and I am so grateful. Thank God!" I exclaimed.

"Don't thank God," my atheistic boss said in a calm voice, "God didn't bring you the food; I did. But don't even thank me."

My schedule at the plant, which began at 8:00 each morning, included cleaning the office and preparing the tools for the day's work. I spent about three weeks learning to use the tools necessary for the job, then was deemed fit to solder electrical connections to underground cables. After a full day's work, I returned to our barracks each day at 6:00 P.M.

My boss gave me plenty of food, but there is physical as well as psychological hunger. Even after I ate my fill, I was still hungry, because I had visions of not having food on the morrow. In that sense, I was always hungry.

Trouble and hunger bring out the instinct of survival, as well as the desire to help another suffering human being in the hope that he will help you. My camp mate, Glickman, who worked for Herr Blum, was a compulsive chain smoker. Thinking of his need and hunger, I said, "Glickman, let's make a deal to share what we have so that neither of us will go hungry. I will give you half the extra food I receive, and you do likewise. Also, I will save the cigar and cigarette butts from the office and give them to you, since I do not smoke. It is a deal?" Glickman shook my hand and agreed.

Thereafter, I would bring my extra portion of bread and share it with Glickman, but I was surprised and saddened that Glickman never seemed to obtain extra food to share with me. Glickman always complained about his boss, Herr Blum, saying that he never spoke to Glickman and never gave him extra food.

The Nazis soon transferred Herr Sträter to the Russian front where his duties in electrical installation continued. The chief superintendent, Herr Krämer, called Glickman and me into his office. He told us that he would soon have to dismiss one of us, because one craftsman required only one helper. "Herr Blum will work with both of you," he said, "and he will decide which one he wants to keep."

I remained for several days at the warehouse, with orders to straighten it up and put the wire and tools in their proper places, while Glickman continued to work for Herr Blum. At the end of the week, Herr Blum stopped me and said, "As of today, you will work with me for a few days and Glickman will do your work. We'll see what kind of worker you are." Herr Blum surprised me with his friendly and talkative nature. He even gave me something to eat during our break. Later that morning, my new boss asked what I thought of Glickman.

"He is a fine fellow," I replied.

"He doesn't say anything good about you," said Herr Blum. "He is constantly degrading your workmanship and your personality."

I was shocked. "I don't know why he would say bad things about me," I continued. "I never did Glickman any harm.

Our deal is to share any extra food we get with each other, but he says you never give him any."

Herr Blum reflected a minute and then said, "I have already decided who to keep as my helper. I can see the difference in character and workmanship. As of next week, I will no longer need Glickman to work for my company. You will be working for me."

So it was. My new boss was a gentleman who trained me and appreciated my work. To my delight, he always gave me food, as he had done for Glickman, who had lied to me. (My stomach was filled but my mind was still hungry.) They assigned Glickman to a new job—digging the ditches in which to place the cables that I would connect.

Glickman had a bitter pill to swallow, and it choked him. Here was the "big man from the big city" who could not be humbled. He soon escaped and was caught. I later heard through the grapevine that, after a few weeks of imprisonment, he was gassed and cremated.

Good Germans

Although the Germans imprisoned us for economic benefits and treated us cruelly, not all Germans were evil. Many individual Germans were humane and compassionate. The help I received from a few of these good Germans was certainly a factor in my survival.

Herr Blum was one such German, and it was a pleasure working for him. Luck brought another one back into my life. Word circulated that my former boss, Herr Sträter, had finished his tour of duty in Russia and would return to manage a work crew as before. The news delighted me because the Nazis had just transferred Herr Blum away from Camp Dretz; I would have been without a job, which meant being without food and life, had it not been for Herr Sträter. He liked me, and my hopes were realized as soon as he returned. He reemployed me to work for him as before.

It was good to work with Herr Sträter again. He told me about some of his experiences while away and asked about my family.

"I saw them last when I escaped Kutno Ghetto," I explained. "There was a typhus epidemic in the ghetto, and I haven't heard from them in well over a year. Even though I still have hope, I'm afraid that they are dead." It was difficult to admit to myself, or to anyone else, that I had probably lost my family forever.

When I related the sad facts, he turned pale and looked at me with compassion and said words I shall never forget: "In times such as these, it is a disgrace to be a German. Please forgive me for such cruelties that some Germans are doing."

Our routine gave us Saturday afternoon and all day Sunday off regular work. On one of these days, Herr Sträter asked if I would be willing to go to his mistress's home and help with some of the chores there. He treated me so wonderfully that I was eager to reciprocate. In addition, I knew that I would have extra food, which meant so much to me in these times of hunger and shortage.

The following Saturday, Herr Sträter obtained permission from the camp commandant and took me to Frau Fenkel's home. Her husband was far away, running a post office for the Germans in Poland. Frau Fenkel invited me—despite my *Judenstern* patches—to sit at the table with them as an equal. She placed the best of food before me and urged me to help myself to my heart's content. When I finished the home-baked buns and pastries, filled with homemade jellies and preserves, I sighed happily. After a time of relaxation, she politely asked if I'd had enough to eat, to which I replied, "Yes, thank you. The food was delicious."

Following some friendly small talk, I felt obliged to return the favors. I politely asked if there were some chores I could do to help her. This pleased my boss, and he winked at me for my tactful gesture, as they were eager to be left alone.

I began sweeping and cleaning the yards, chopping wood, and doing whatever I could to help. I fed the horse, the cow, and the chickens. I cleaned and straightened the barn to perfection. This routine went on for several weekends.

One Saturday afternoon, Frau Fenkel approached me with a smiling glint in her eyes. She told me that her niece, whom she had raised, had been away at school and would soon return to live with her. The next Saturday afternoon, I had the pleasure of meeting Hilda. After we exchanged smiles, Frau Fenkel said that we would be doing the chores together.

One of the first things I did—perhaps to impress Hilda with my masculinity—was to chop some wood for the fire. Hilda looked on with respect and amazement. The more she watched, the better I chopped. The ax repeatedly split the wood in two pieces, as though I were an expert. One chop, two pieces, one chop, two pieces.

Hilda approached me and admiringly said, "Just let me try that!" She tried, but her muscles and frame were built for more sensitive pursuits. Nature had endowed her well, but not for chopping wood. Hilda took the ax, raised it with difficulty, and let it fall into the wood without splitting the logs. I then had to help her extract the embedded ax from the wood. I held her white, soft hands and felt her warm breath near me as I came to her help at her request.

Hilda was a determined Fraülein. She wanted to impress me and prove herself, so she did not give up. Again and again, Hilda tried to split the logs as she saw me do so easily. Again and again, I sought to be near her, to put her hand in mine, to help her extract the ax that had failed to do its work. Hilda came up to me eye to eye—and tempting lips to lips—and said worshipfully, "You are a strong and very skilled, almost professional woodsman. Could that be your trade?" she asked in a melting tone.

I smiled. "The war unfortunately interrupted my schooling, and I had to learn many skills the hard way." Hilda enjoyed my company and sought every opportunity to be near me. I certainly didn't fight it. She was like a breath of fresh air for me, as the Nazis had kept me cooped up for well over a year without being close to the opposite sex.

"Why don't we saw some wood together?" Hilda suggested. I was now walking toward the barn for the saw upon feet that were as light as air. We sawed together, pulling to and fro, as we stared at each other all the while. I do not know what excited her as she looked toward me, a short and skinny prisoner, but before me was a shapely, sexy Fraülein in a low-cut blouse. Her to and fro movements only inflamed me further. The sawing motion rhythmically exposed her breasts, and I had to control my thoughts, my feelings, and my emotions. She was German, and I was Jewish. It was a golden opportunity for both of us, but it was a temptation to which I could only say no.

I was as happy and carefree as I could possibly be that summer, considering the circumstances, especially on weekends. I was never hungry for food—but Hilda was a feast I was never to have.[1]

Fall came and with it the harvest.[2] Bringing in the crops was a high priority, and there was a shortage of labor. I was assigned to help a nearby farmer with his harvest. Luck brought me to the farm of Wilhelm Schultz, an elderly gentleman whose son and son-in-law were in the military. He and his daughter tried very hard to run the farm and harvest the desperately needed crops, but they couldn't manage without help. Upon my arrival, they greeted me warmly and respectfully. They sincerely appreciated my help and told me so. It was good again to feel like a human being in the presence of other human beings.

My first task was to harvest potatoes behind a horse-drawn potato digger. As the horse moved forward, the potatoes rose to the surface of the soil. Very quickly and rhythmically, I had to bend down, pick up the potatoes and place them into a basket. I had never done this type of work before. It was hard and backbreaking, especially because I wanted to do my best not to miss any potatoes buried in the earth.

Herr Schultz came to know me as a good worker and treated me as a friend. He inquired about my past and shared news with me of his own family. Like Herr Sträter, it shocked Herr Schultz to learn that the Germans could so mistreat innocent people. The fact that I was Jewish did not influence him negatively. I enjoyed helping Herr Schultz, and I often did extra work, without being asked, just to show my appreciation.

1. From eye-witness reports smuggled out of Europe, by the summer of 1942, Allied nations had detailed information concerning the extermination of European Jews. On June 2 the BBC (British Broadcasting Company) broadcast extracts from a report telling of the extermination of 700,000 Jews at Chelmno and elsewhere. On August 8, 1942, Gerhard Riegner, the World Jewish Congress representative in Geneva, sent a telegram to both the British and American governments with information about the "Final Solution." In response to such reports, an inter-Allied declaration was issued on November 17, 1942, denouncing the murder of European Jewry and stating that those responsible would be punished. However, no direct action was taken to halt or slow the killing process. And on April 19, 1943 (the same day as the beginning of the Warsaw Ghetto uprising), American and British officials, at a conference in Bermuda, failed to implement plans for the rescue of European Jews or to provide assistance for Jewish refugees.

2. In mid-November 1942, the deportation of German Gypsies to Auschwitz began.

I shall never forget his remark to me in an attempt to boost my morale. "I guarantee you," he said, "that if our Führer Hitler could only see you work and see the fine person you are, he would never harm a hair on your head. Instead, he would reward you." I paused in silence. Knowing what Herr Schultz in his innocence had been brainwashed to believe, there was nothing for me to say.

I was the envy of many at the camp because Herr Schultz so generously rewarded me with food. Routinely, after about an hour's work, everybody stopped to rest and have some hot tea and rolls. The Schultz family always invited me to join them for the noon meal, usually vegetable soup with meat and bread. It was delicious and filling. We would stop each day at about 3:00 for vespers (afternoon prayers) and a snack. Before I left at 5:30 each day, they would give me a package of food to take home, and they would bid me farewell each day with a friendly pat on the back.

The week before Christmas 1942, Herr Schultz told me to be sure to come to his farm for Christmas—but not to work. I remember being led to the Schultz family Christmas tree. Under the tree was a package for me! I was so excited to see what was in it. I was as impatient as a child. After enjoying a fine meal with the family, they gave me the gaily decorated package. "Take this home with you," Herr Schultz said. "Enjoy it, my friend, and Happy Christmas to you."

It was a happy Christmas for me. When I returned to camp, I waited until I was alone and then eagerly opened the package. Inside, I found several pairs of new socks and a spanking new shirt, so badly needed and so difficult to obtain. There were also food delicacies, including assorted sausages, loaves of homemade bread, and cookies. A cake with "Merry Christmas, Abram" inscribed in chocolate icing was more than enough to bring tears of joy and appreciation to my eyes. I thanked God for watching over me and for the good people that I had the fortune to meet.

Sadly, this was my last visit with Herr Schultz. The German war effort must have embittered the High Command, because orders came from Berlin forbidding Jews to leave the camp except as forced labor.[3]

My work at the factory with Herr Sträter continued happily, without incident, until the day he asked me to go to the Sumens factory to get a bucket of water. I filled the bucket and, as I was leaving, the superintendent of the building stopped me. As he stared at my *Judenstern* patches, he growled, "Jew, who gives you the right to violate this building with your presence?"

"I'm simply carrying out my boss's orders," I explained. "He asked me to fill this bucket with water."

The superintendent grew furious and, without warning, he grabbed me by the neck and gave me a powerful shove. I fell uncontrollably down two flights of stairs, and the water spilled everywhere. Dazed, I had no choice but to return with my empty bucket and wet clothes.

When Herr Sträter learned what had happened, he froze in disbelief, hung his head in shame, and exclaimed, "One has to be really ashamed to be a German. How unbelievable that this could happen in our cultured land!"

Several weeks later, as I was soldering a cable, the same Sumens superintendent came by. My insides trembled when I saw him coming toward me, not knowing just what he would do. I knew he hated Jews with a passion. He stopped to watch me work. He nodded approvingly and, as if nothing had previously happened between us, started a conversation. "You, of all people, should pray now and hope that we Germans win the war. If we don't," he said, "our enemies will kill all you Jews. If we win, we will always need good workers like you. We will only castrate you so that you will be sterile. You will have peace knowing that you are working for the betterment of the Master Race." He walked away. I paused and thought, God forbid that I should live to see the Germans win the war and use me as their lifelong sterile slave. When he left, I was angry but relieved that not all Germans were like him.

The day had its brighter side. Waiting for me when I returned to camp was a letter from Ester Rosenthal, my secret flame from the Krosniewice Ghetto. I opened it eagerly.

3. By early November 1942, the tide of war had turned against the Nazis with the British victory at El Alamein, Egypt, followed by the Russian counter-attack at Stalingrad.

Dear Abe,

By a miracle, I learned your address. I pray that you get this note. It means so much to me to be able to write to you. How are things for you? Your cousin, Gucia, and I are at a prison camp for women. It is terrible here. We have to dig ditches every day in our bare feet, up to our knees in mud. What little food we get isn't fit to eat. There is no one here that we know. I can't believe what's happening to us.

My shoes wore out a long time ago, and they won't give me another pair. I need a new pair of shoes desperately. If you could help me in any way, I'd remember your kindness forever.

Love,
Ester

I did not sleep well that night. The next morning, I related the situation to Herr Sträter, and he agreed to help me. Two days later, he obtained a pair of women's boots. He placed them in a package, along with some food for both Ester and Gucia. Knowing the German mind, he mailed the package to Ester with a fictitious return address. I was extremely grateful for his help.

I sat down and recalled my happy experience in the bread line with Ester in Krosniewice, Poland. Her pretty face, her sparkling black eyes framed by blue-black braids, and her youthful, sexy figure flashed in my memory's eyes. How happy I would have been, embracing her, but the world was in flames, life was uncertain, and Ester was far away.

I took paper and pencil in hand and wrote to Ester about the package, telling her to be on the lookout and to enjoy it. I decided to seize this opportunity and share my inner feelings for her, knowing that the chances were slim that we would ever see each other again. I wrote in detail of my love for her. After several pages, I closed with a prayer over her, and I encouraged her not to lose her hope and courage. The truth is good to say and good to know.

Auschwitz

Spring came and nature began her floral dance. With spring came hope that things were getting better. Despite my high hopes, however, April 1943 brought me to a life-and-death crisis. Only a few of us had heard the dark destiny that lurked ahead—perhaps this is the Lord's Wisdom. If we had known all at once what grief and danger lay ahead, the burden would have crushed us.[1]

I had been happily working for Herr Sträter, a man of high stature. Working for him meant working with him. The time I spent at the factory was most pleasant. It made me feel like a human being to work, to learn, and to earn my keep.

It was a Wednesday morning, and I cheerfully headed for work, as usual. This day, however, was to be different. Herr Sträter's face was sad. "Herr Meister," I asked, my heart pounding, "did I do anything wrong?"

"No, Abe," my boss replied. "You did nothing wrong. Today we are going to do no work at all. You and I are going to bicycle around so that we can enjoy the day together. I heard rumors—only rumors—that they are shipping you out to a faraway labor camp."

I was speechless. I was dumbfounded. My body trembled with the foreboding of fear. The entire atmosphere was saturated with sadness and heavy, unknown, dreary destiny. My throat was dry, and I could not speak; my eyes were dry, and I could not cry.

1. On April 19, 1943, the Warsaw Ghetto uprising began as Nazis initiated the final liquidation of the ghetto. By the end of May 1943 the entire ghetto was destroyed.

"Dear God," I prayerfully sobbed in my heart, "what will the future bring? What troubles lie ahead for me? Why am I being punished so?"

Here, they treated me like a human being. I earned my bread with dignity. I had grown accustomed to my surroundings and the routine. I hated the thought of leaving Herr Sträter. My day with him ended all too soon. We took leave of one another with a friendly handshake and an embrace. Our hearts told us that we would never see each other again.

When I returned to camp, we received our orders: "Attention!" the local speaker blared out, "Early tomorrow morning, this entire camp will be transferred to a distant location. Pack all of your belongings, and be ready to move. We will give you a ration of food for the trip."

I spent the night lying in bed with my eyes wide open, seized with fear of the unknown. Morning came, and the guards hustled us onto trucks. They hauled us to the waiting cattle cars at the railroad station. They crammed about fifty of us into each car and locked the doors. We felt like animals in cages. There were no sanitary provisions. There was only straw on the floor for us to sit on, to urinate on, to defecate on—to die on. After three days' confinement without light, with only a trickle of air, the stench was incredibly horrid. We covered our feces and urine with the available straw in one corner. Sleeping was impossible. We had to try to sleep in a sitting position, as there was never enough room to stretch out on the floor.

Our train finally came to a screeching halt. Someone unlocked and opened the doors. It was good for a moment to feel and breathe the fresh air. It was an exhilarating feeling, but after a breath or two, we were greeted with angry shouts. "*Heraus, ihr Hunde!* (Out, you dogs!)." Surrounding us were SS guards and officers in their crisp uniforms, aiming their pistols, rifles, and machine guns at us. Some held back police dogs that wanted to tear us apart. Sounds of wailing and shouting filled the air. It was a terrifying spectacle. It had the smell of death, and we trembled with fear.

We were at the now infamous railroad landing at Camp

Birkenau, Poland, part of the Auschwitz complex.[2] Out we marched as ordered, with guns still pointing at us from all sides. The Nazis ordered us into lines for selection. Fortunately, because we were in decent health while working out of Camp Dretz, we all survived the trip and passed selection. Little did we know how many innocent human beings had been given the death sentence upon arriving at Birkenau, after no more than a glance by the Nazis.

They then marched us through the gates and shoved us into dark, dreary horse stables that had been converted into barracks. They crammed about thirty prisoners into each stall, originally intended for no more than three horses. A tall, muscular Jewish prisoner strutted by and showed off his large club, the symbol of his authority.

"You have not come to paradise!" he thundered. "Here you will do exactly as you are told, with no questions, or else! These are your beds. Choose one now." The *Stubenälteste* (prisoner assigned the responsibility of the room and its prisoners) pointed to the three-tier bunk beds that we were to occupy. I quickly climbed to the uppermost level and made this my bunk. Again, my bunk choice turned out to be a wise one. Our *Stubenälteste* wielded his club many times just to show his dictatorial authority, inflicting bruises and fractures for no reason at all.

We had to get permission to use the outside toilet. Our *Stubenälteste* only gave his permission when he felt like it, and he often did not feel like it. For begging a second time, I was rewarded with his club. We spent that night in total fear. Our *Stubenälteste* had not lied to us. It was no paradise—it was hell.

Our *Stubenälteste* ordered us to divest ourselves of all belongings, except our clothing. "Can I please keep my family pictures?" I begged.

His reply was terse and direct. "Where you are going, you won't need any pictures. You won't need anything."

2. Auschwitz began in 1940 as a concentration camp for Poles and then Soviet POW's. It became a death camp for Jews in 1941-42 when another camp, called Auschwitz II, was built at Birkenau. Birkenau housed five gas chambers, and between April 1942 and November 1944 it exterminated more than 6,000 Soviet POW's, about as many Gypsies, and around 1.5 million Jews.

On the following morning, we marched a few kilometers to another camp. Any camp would be better than this, I thought. In front of us, we saw a large gate with a sign that read, ARBEIT MACHT FREI (Work Brings Freedom). We were at Auschwitz Concentration Camp, in Oswiecim, Poland. My eyes roved over the new site. The camp we had just left was dilapidated and almost knee-high in mud. Here, at Auschwitz, I saw paved streets and many two-story buildings, surrounded by a double row of high barbed-wire fences. A sign on the fence read, *Vorsicht Hochspannung* (Caution, High Voltage). Towers armed with SS guards were strategically positioned throughout the camp.

The Germans marched us into a tall building where they gave us a towel and a cake of soap. They made us discard all of our clothing and march into the shower room. As we exited the shower room, they gave us shoes and striped prison uniforms that did not fit. We made do as best we could by trading with each other for better fits. It was a compromise. When I first saw men wearing these uniforms, I naively remarked to my buddy, "It could not be so bad if people are allowed to walk around in their pajamas."

Ahead of us on the outside were many lines of prisoners. They ordered us to line up by alphabet. Some lines were for names beginning A–F, others for G–K, and so on. When my turn came, I stood face to face with another prisoner who held a tattoo needle and paper. "Stretch out your left arm," he said in a tired voice, and he went to work. We were too tired and frightened to resist. "From now on, you must remember this number. Your name doesn't mean a thing anymore." In less than five minutes, I lost my identity as a prisoner with a name and became just #124157. As a Jew, I received the bonus decoration of a triangle tattooed under the number on the back of my left forearm. For Jews, the tattoo was an added insult, because tattoos are forbidden by Jewish law.

Like army recruits going through a line, we visited the various stations for processing. A prisoner was waiting to write my new number neatly on the white cloth label sewn to my jacket. Another one sewed a patch on my shirt beneath my number. It consisted of a red triangle pointing down, indicating

that I was a political prisoner, crossed by a yellow triangle pointing up to form the Star of David. Each category of prisoner had
a different color. The color yellow symbolized degradation—
a special present for "Jews only."[3]

The Auschwitz officials assigned us to large brick barracks, called
Blocks. We were quarantined for ten days to determine if any
of us were disease carriers. Without losing any time, they
called us to assembly on the eleventh day and asked whether
we were common or specialized laborers. I claimed to be an electrician and was assigned to the Auschwitz bakery, located outside the camp, to install lighting.

Each morning, many thousands of us made our exit through
the Auschwitz gates under the watchful eyes of the SS, who were
armed with loaded rifles pointed at us. It took about one and
one-half hours for all the forced laborers to pass through the
gates. As we marched, the Germans tried to motivate us with
beautiful music, played by a forty-piece orchestra made up of
the most talented prisoners. They played the peppiest march
melodies from around the world, including American composers
such as John Philip Sousa. We learned to march in cadence as
our officers called out, "*Links-zwei-drei-vier.* (Left-two-three-
four)." We learned to march like professional soldiers. As we
marched by the gates, German officers on both sides inspect-
ed us for neatness and cleanliness. Severe punishment awaited
those men whose numbers were recorded because of untidy uniforms or dirty shoes.

The average prisoner was underfed and rigorously driven in
extremely hard work. Some were forced to unload tons of
brick and clay for the construction of munitions factories.
They had to work without rest and were always in fear of the
whip.

Happily, eight of us spent a few weeks installing the lighting
in the Auschwitz Bakery, located outside the camp. We could

3. Uniforms bore triangles of different colors: green for professional criminals,
red for political opposition, black for prostitutes and other "asocials," pink for
homosexuals, purple for fundamentalist "exponents of the Bible." Otto Friedrich,
The Kingdom of Auschwitz (New York: HarperPerennial, 1994), p. 34.

eat all the bread we desired while working. They even allowed us to take half a loaf of bread back to camp as a reward for good work. Most others were not so lucky.

After that, I ended up in the common labor pool. They assigned me to work with Polish civilians, skilled masons who were constructing various factories. I had to toss bricks up to another prisoner on a scaffold, who arranged them into piles for the masons to use. Handling the rough-edged bricks left my bare hands raw, bleeding, and blistered. I soon developed calloused hands so that handling bricks was no longer such a problem.

The Germans used every available technique to squeeze the most work from their prison labor force. The German war effort was faltering by October 1943. Time to the Germans was of the essence, and orders came down to drive us hard.[4]

The Germans accelerated the pace in the camp. To increase productivity, the Nazis devised an incentive program of points for extra work and extra effort. For example, if a prisoner worked harder, his overseer might give him several points. They put up a chart to track our progress. For several points, a prisoner could get an extra piece of bread. For several more points, he could get a pack of cigarettes. For enough accumulated points, the reward might even be spending the night with a woman. This particular incentive, however, was only for non-Jewish prisoners. So little did the Germans esteem the person of a Jewish woman that they never drafted Jewish women as slaves for this particular purpose. It seems that the Germans considered a Christian prisoner of war too fine to be demeaned and insulted by sleeping with a Jew.

The Nazis had assigned several Jewish prisoners in our block to work in the *Kanada*, a large warehouse used to store the clothing and possessions of prisoners who were executed. It was their job to sort the belongings of Jewish victims that were murdered in the gas chambers of Birkenau. Some of my friends were able

4. As already noted, the war effort actually had begun failing in late 1942. Heinrich Himmler, who organized the SS (Protection Squad), reacted in June 1943: he set up slave-labor battalions to exhume and burn corpses at death camps and execution sites throughout Poland and Russia in order to hide evidence of the Holocaust.

to steal jewelry and other valuables that were small enough to carry in their mouths or under their clothes. They wanted to trade these items with Polish civilians on the outside, with whom we were in contact. We bartered a pair of earrings, a watch, or a few coins for bread, butter, eggs, cigarettes, and other items on the black market. To be caught by the Germans—stealing from the Nazis and trading with the Poles—meant certain death, but not to do so meant not to survive.

I used these stolen goods in various ways. On one occasion, I had learned through contacts that I was on a list to be transferred from Auschwitz to a coal mining detail. This meant that I would be shackled with chains and forced to work in a dark, damp mine. Death was certain after a short period of time in these conditions. By trading some cigarettes and soap, I was able to have my name removed from that list. Bribing my overseers to improve my situation in the camps became almost routine.

Our *Kapo*, or foreman, was an old German criminal prisoner. He wore a prison uniform with a green triangle, identifying him as a criminal prisoner rather than a political prisoner. He was just as hungry and miserable as we were—and even more wretched. Because he was a German, though, they entrusted him to be our foreman. They placed a whip and a cane at his disposal. He used them cruelly, whenever the spirit moved him. He was in full charge on Saturday afternoons because the civilian skilled labor did not work. On these days, he showed his true spirit, which was ugly and mean.

Our *Kapo* was a heavy smoker and, like us, he was always hungry. It occurred to me that a little bribe might sweeten him up and get him off our backs. In desperation, I conceived a plan. Perhaps bolder than most, I took my chances and gave our abusive *Kapo* a pack of Ergo, Polish cigarettes. He took them with a smile and asked no questions. We continued to bribe our *Kapo* daily with food, cigarettes, or soap. He became a sweetened man, as are all bribed men. Our *Kapo* now owed us, and our Saturday afternoons became our own—to rest and recuperate from a hard week of work. Our *Kapo* retreated a distance from us and left us alone.

This happy arrangement went on for weeks, until one Saturday, when our *Kapo* came over to me and sadistically hit me on the head with his cane. For absolutely no reason, he pushed me until I fell on the ground, and I hit my head on the push-cart rail. In a youthful, uncontrolled rage, I rushed my attacker and pushed him with all my might against a rail cart, without thinking of the consequences. (I forgot that death might be my punishment for this momentary satisfaction.) The *Kapo's* jacket got caught on the cart, which rolled away and dragged him several yards. He was in a helpless and demeaning position. He quickly pulled himself together and angrily shouted, "I am going to report you, and this will be your last punishment."

I made a last-ditch effort and confidently said, "I know that if you report me, there will be no hope for me. I assure you, though, that I will not die alone. When I tell the German authorities that you took bribes from us all these months, you will dangle from the noose alongside me."

The *Kapo* quickly calmed down and changed his tone, saying, "Even though I am burning mad, I am going to forget what happened. I am going to punish you, however, by having you transferred out of my work crew." I didn't want to show my excitement, but this was much more a reward than punishment.

The following Monday I began working with another crew and a new *Kapo*, Herr Braun. Like my former *Kapo*, Herr Braun was a German criminal prisoner. He was in his thirties and very handsome, with dark hair. Unlike my former *Kapo*, Herr Braun was our friend. He had an open mind and repeatedly told us that he was in the same fix that we were in.

Despite his German background, Herr Braun felt the pain of others and considered himself one of us. When evening came and our work detail was over, he sat and talked with us. We exchanged common hopes and aspirations.

I had the added pleasure of learning that my old friend, Abram Danziger, was in my new work crew. He joined us in our evening discussions. I used to think that the greatest moment would be when I could properly return the kindness and repay Chaim Arnavi, who had helped me and nursed me back to health after my beating by the German gendarmes in the Krosniewice Ghetto. Abram Danziger also deserved my thanks for helping me recover then, when I was caught attempting to smuggle some food into the ghetto where my parents and two sisters were confined.

The Nazis soon assigned one of the men who lived in our barracks to work as a painter at Camp Birkenau. While working in the women's section, many inmates approached him and asked for favors. Out of all the inmates at Birkenau, two girls approached him and asked if he knew of a man at Auschwitz named Abram Korn.

One of the girls turned out to be my cousin, Gucia Korn. She was the sister of Jacob, who went berserk and stole out of Camp Hardt, taking only his blanket. The other girl was Ester Rosenthal, who lit a flame in my heart over two years earlier in the Krosniewice Ghetto. I was enamored with her and had arranged to put her near the front of a bread line. It was a brief moment of unreciprocated passion, but I believe she never forgot. From the letter I sent her while I was in Camp Dretz, she knew of my love for her.

Ester was again hungry for food, and she sent me a message asking for help. Her plea touched me, and I resolved to do what I could to help her. Food was not plentiful, but, because of my contact with Polish civilians, I was able to secure a little extra bread.

I asked the painter, David Reich, to take the girls a few slices of this bread. When David returned that night, he described the scene. "It was a battle," David said. "Your cousin, Gucia, grabbed the food away from Ester and shouted, 'You are no relative. You do not deserve any food from Abe Korn. Give me that bread!'" It distressed me to hear that Ester was so humiliated. Fortunately, David recovered the bread from Gucia and gave it back to Ester.

Gucia and Ester had endured much hardship and shared many months of friendship together. Certainly, during these lean years, they had learned to help one another and share their food supply, or they could not have survived. Gucia was normally a caring, sweet girl, but hunger and deprivation robs one of dignity and concern for others. They lived in a bitterly dehumanizing setting. Gucia's animal instinct had apparently triumphed over her better nature. It was indeed difficult to be humane in an atmosphere where "might makes right" was a way of life.

As a result, I began packaging the slices of bread into two separate wrappings. For the next week, David maintained contact with the girls and shared the bread equally between them. During this short time, it comforted me to know that they had a little extra bread to eat.

It was a sad day for me when David was no longer able to bring news of my cousin and my old flame. I do not know what happened to them after David lost contact with them. I had lost my parents and my sisters. By helping these girls, I felt that I was still in touch with part of my family. Now that this avenue had closed, I felt alone—all alone in a cruel, dark, cold world. Even the clouds that obscured the sun spoke to me of sadness.

Kapo Braun did his best to take us out of the misery that we were in. He tried to raise our sagging spirits by teaching us different German marching songs. Most of us could speak only a little German. It required much time and patience to teach us the words and melodies that we ended up singing and enjoying. "*Ein Heller und Ein Batzen* (A Penny and a Silver Coin)" was one of our favorite songs.

One night Kapo Braun reluctantly told us that our assignment with Polish civilians was at an end. We would now have to do roofing work in a nearby German installation. This, of course, meant that our source of extra food from Polish civilians had dried up—and so would we if we didn't come up with another way to get food.

Each day, we rolled drums of tar to the sites of the leaky roofs and went to work repairing the cracks. Our daily march took us by a large, mysterious building, which we learned was a warehouse containing food, soap, cigarettes, and other luxuries. It was a distribution center for all the nearby German camps.

The Germans devised a devilish scheme. Each morning, the Germans marched more than fifty men into this warehouse and gave them their assignment for the day—to pack and sort the various commodities as ordered on the worksheets. They searched the prisoners before they entered and before they left, and locked them inside all day long. In this way the Germans were sure that these prisoners could have, at worst, filled their stomachs with food, but could take nothing out. The prisoners who worked in the warehouse were eager to take some of the supplies outside. We, in turn, were eager to obtain some of the extra supplies, but were never allowed inside. We connived to learn the identity of these men and to collaborate with them.

We soon learned that four of the men who lived in our barracks worked inside the warehouse. We met with them and, like the Germans, devised a plan. Each day, at noon break, our work detail would arrange to wander discreetly near the window where the workers were stationed. At our signal, a whistle, the four men inside would begin throwing out supplies.

We now faced the problem of smuggling our soon-to-be stolen goods into camp without being caught. Some welders, who worked in the repair shop, made a false bottom in one of the barrels we used to carry tar. We would place the ill-gotten goods in this hidden compartment and cover the false bottom with tar, giving the appearance of a full barrel of tar.

The day came for our first attempt. We wandered up to the window and gave the secret whistle. Within seconds, large quantities of food, soap, cigarettes, and other items came flying out of the window. Our friends were a little overenthused this first day. It was almost too much to fit into the barrel.

We nonchalantly rolled the barrel back through the gates and into the camp. When the moment was right, we opened it up and shared its contents, especially rewarding the four welders who helped us. We also shared our booty with a few other workers from the warehouse to keep them quiet.

We managed to arrange for our guard not to see us at first. When he began to wonder what we were doing, we bribed him to keep him quiet. This satisfied him, and he winked at our operation, not wanting to know exactly how we obtained the gifts. We soon had to bribe other German guards, and we continued our scheme for several weeks.

Resistance

Resistance entered the mind of every prisoner of war, and certainly of every Jew, who suffered at the hands of the Nazis. Most Jews detested their oppressors, but relatively few actively resisted them. The Polish underground, however, played a vital role in resisting our Nazi oppressors, as did many courageous individuals.[1]

Living in Auschwitz, we would have been completely cut off from reality, and from any hope, had it not been for the Polish underground. Many members of the underground risked their lives to infiltrate our camp and live with us in our despicable surroundings. Most of us did not know their identities. Disclosure of such knowledge would have meant torture and death, for them as well as for us. The underground somehow managed to bring in news of the outside world, of German defeats and successes in battle, and of the whereabouts of partisans who were fighting to help us. They gave us hope that something would soon happen to take us out of our misery.

When the Germans took the routine head count upon returning to camp, there occasionally would be one or two people missing. We then knew that underground members had made their

---

1. Both armed and unarmed resistance, by Jews and non-Jews alike, took place throughout the Holocaust, thwarting the ultimate goal of the Nazis' "Final Solution." Noteworthy, among others, are: Raoul Wallenberg, a Swedish diplomat in Budapest who, in November 1944, personally intervened to save thousands of Hungarian Jews destined for the gas chambers; Oskar Schindler, a member of the Nazi party who put Jews to work in his enamelware factory and saved more than 1,100 lives; and the people of the small Protestant village of Le Chambon, France, where more than 5,000 Jewish children were hidden from the Nazis between 1940 and 1944.

escape. This would always infuriate our Nazi overlords, and would secretly delight us.

Underground members were bold and took many risks, some of which succeeded before our eyes. A curious situation took place one evening. The Germans conducted their regular head count when we returned from our day of toil. The count totaled 78, when there were only to be 77 men. There was one *extra* man. He was obviously a member of the underground who had infiltrated our camp. The Germans did everything they could to filter out the intruder. One guard called each man to step forward, one at a time, while another guard watched us very closely. Somehow, and I do not understand how to this day, when the guards finished calling out the last prisoner's number, there was no one left standing. The weary German officers concluded that their count must have been in error. One extra man didn't concern them as much as one missing man. This episode closed, and the underground member was later able to escape unharmed.

Even Nazi officers were among underground members and cooperated in various ways to thwart the German Master Plan. Two such German officers had the difficult task of smuggling out two prisoners. These courageous men hid the prisoners in clothes hampers that contained clean bed linen to be shipped to German army installations. Someone tipped off the German command, and they stopped the linen truck at the gate. They found the hidden prisoners and immediately arrested the German officers. Within minutes, the Nazis placed these courageous officers in solitary confinement, along with the prisoners they had tried to help. The Nazis interrogated, tortured, and finally murdered all four men.

On another occasion, as we marched to work one morning, two high-ranking German officers stopped us. They presented our guard with papers ordering him to turn over two prisoners from our work detail. When we returned to camp that evening, we learned that the officers were members of the underground, posed in stolen uniforms. They had freed two of their own who had been with us in Auschwitz.

The Germans methodically robbed their victims of strength and the will to resist, with brutal psychological and physical tactics. First they took all rights away from the Jews. Then they confiscated their homes, their businesses, and all their possessions. They herded the Jews into cattle cars, with little light and air. Sanitary facilities were nonexistent. A horrible stench poisoned the lungs of the weary travelers. By the time the prisoners arrived at their destinations, usually after several days without food or water, these tortured people became subservient, and the idea of a shower was heavenly to them. Many were those who willingly but unknowingly walked to their death in the "showers."

It took one beautiful Jewish woman destined for the "showers" to write a chapter in the history of courage and resistance. In the summer of 1943,[2] the Germans brought in a transport of Italian Jews to Birkenau. The cattle-car train, like thousands of others before it, rolled up to the Birkenau landing, part of the Auschwitz complex. On this particular train load, there was an actress in her early twenties. Those who saw her described her as radiant in youth and ravishing in beauty. She walked with pride and stood out in a crowd. When the German SS men saw her, sexual fever rose in their eyes. The Nazis ordered the mixed group of men, women, and children into the "shower room." SS men, stationed on the outside of a huge steel door, were regular witnesses and supervisors of mass execution. It was their job and bizarre pleasure to watch through a peephole in the door to ascertain that the poison gas had done its job well and that their victims were dead.

One of the SS men watched with unholy and devilish glee as the prisoners stood there, naked, and his eye beheld the Italian

2. Spring/summer 1943 saw many acts of resistance. In April, the month Abe entered Auschwitz-Birkenau, the Warsaw Ghetto uprising succeeded in holding back the German army for a little over a month. During the summer, the Nazis liquidated every ghetto in Polish and Russian territory with the exception of the Lodz Ghetto, which remained until August 1944. In many of these ghettos, Jews resisted as they learned the true meaning of "deportation."

Rebellions also occurred in many camps. The prisoners revolted at the Treblinka death camp on August 2, 1943, resulting in the escape of about 200 prisoners (only 12 survived), and hastening the camp's closing and dismantling. A revolt at the Sobibor death camp, where about 600 escaped on October 14, 1943 (only about half survived), resulted in the decision to dismantle and entirely demolish the camp.

actress. While the others had followed orders and undressed, she simply stood there, fully clothed, in all her voluptuous beauty. She realized that the Nazis intended some other evil besides a shower, and she would not undress.

The steel door, which would normally open only after death had won out, opened this once at the urge of a living animal masquerading as a human being. In rushed the SS man who had been peeping all along. "Why haven't you undressed for the shower like the others?" he shouted as he moved toward her in a rage.

With dignity and head held high, this beautiful woman calmly explained, "I am a lady, and I fail to see why I should undress in front of strange men."

"Because I order you to undress in front of strange men!" he barked, as his eyes roved and searched out the sexual characteristics of her body.

The actress proclaimed sternly, "I will never undress before you!"

The German SS man grabbed the actress in an uncontrollable rage and began tearing her clothes from her body. As she stood, wearing only her panties and bra, with the SS man reaching for her breast, the actress rose to play her last role in this duel with imminent death. In a split second, to the surprise of everyone, she, herself, tore off her bra to use as her only and last weapon. She flung it at the eyes of her attacker, and while he was dazed, surprised, and momentarily blinded, she grabbed the pistol from his holster and shot him dead. Two more SS men rushed in; she killed one and seriously wounded the other.

Wearing only her panties, she ran outside the "shower room" where people lined up to enter. She shouted, "This is no shower! You are all waiting to be murdered!" She then emptied her pistol in the direction of the German guards. Seconds later, the German sentries in the guard tower machine-gunned our actress down. She died in what she must have known was a blaze of glory. The Jewish actress was one of the few who resisted her executioners and also succeeded in becoming their executioner.

The tragic tale of this heroic woman would never have

come to light—dead ones tell no tales—were it not for the *Sonderkommando*. As they waited to do their job of disposing of the corpses, they saw and heard it all. They later shared this news with us.[3]

The commandant of Auschwitz had to avenge this German shame. How could a lowly Jewess dare to resist the Master Race and kill powerful SS men! It was a question of German honor. When we returned from our day's work and walked through the gates of Auschwitz, we saw two black flags hanging low. Fear gripped our hearts. We knew that the Germans were not mourning the death of Jews. Our fears proved to be sadly correct.

The next day, we stood at assembly while the German camp doctor walked through our ranks with his fellow officer, *Unterscharführer* (Technical Sergeant) Kaduk, writing down numbers. The commandant announced the 200 selected numbers over the loudspeakers, and then he dismissed the rest of us. These selected prisoners had to remain standing while the rest of us marched to our barracks. The Nazis then marched the 200 unfortunate Auschwitz prisoners to their deaths because of the efforts of our heroine.

Among those selected for the executioner was Mr. Abbe. Mr. Abbe had been our barracks leader in Camp Dretz, near Berlin. He was a German Jew, selected by the Germans as our overseer. Despite the indignities and imprisonment he suffered at the hands of his fellow countrymen, he refused to believe that the Germans would harm him. He was blindly and stupidly loyal to his last living moment.

Camp life was an unending fight for life, and, for some, a

---

3. This heroine was actually a Polish dancer named Horowitz, not an Italian actress. The story varies from one version to the next, as it was handed down from *Sonderkommandos*, who were probably murdered because they were witnesses. The train held 2,000 wealthy Polish Jews, who had paid millions of dollars for false South American passports (hence the reason some reports claim they were Americans), obtained from the SS by Horowitz. In Italy, the Nazis told them that they would be sent to Switzerland to be exchanged and sent to South America. Instead, the Nazis sent them straight to the gas chambers at Birkenau. The SS guard was Schillinger. Konnilyn Feig, *Hitler's Death Camps* (New York: Holmes and Meier, 1979), pp. 349-51.

fight for freedom. One evening, after we returned from work, the German officers discovered that there was one Polish political prisoner missing. After searching for him, the Germans found no trace of him. They were angry and ashamed. Something had to be done to instill fear into the hearts of the inmates of the camp. The Nazis sought out the escapee's parents. Several days later, as we returned from work, the escapee's parents were there, standing on a platform. They had huge signs hanging around their necks for all to see. We were told to look and we did. The signs in bold letters said, "We are being punished because our stupid son escaped German justice." This was a sad and frightening reminder to us that German retribution and revenge was far reaching. The Nazis wanted us to know that no one could escape the iron claw of the German war machine.

Several days later, another Polish political prisoner escaped. The German guards set out with police dogs to find both escapees. They had trained the dogs to be vicious. The Nazis found the escapees and unleashed the dogs on them. The dogs tore the flesh viciously from the escapees' bodies. Bleeding and dying, they were brought back and placed on the platform for us to see them in their misery as they fought with death. Again, they forced us to look.

With stony faces, we walked by this horrid example of man's inhumanity to man. Our eyes beheld a stomach-turning sight. Blood was oozing from their torn bodies as they lay there, writhing in pain. They begged for death to take them from their misery. On the platform was another sign that read, "This will happen to anyone who tries to outsmart the German Master Race."

We could say nothing and do nothing, or else meet a similar end. We felt much pity in our hearts and compassion for these human beings who were disgraced, dishonored, and left to die just because they wanted to be free. Our hatred of and disgust with German justice and their way of doing things continued to grow.

We had to make do with the circumstances in which we found ourselves. As we looked around and observed other prisoners of war, we found that some of us were not completely dehumanized as others were. We could still think and react as humans. We helped each other and considered our friends as family. We cared about each other, Jews and Christians alike. When there was bread to share, we shared our bread. When there were moments of sorrow, we comforted one another. During the rare moments of happiness, we shared our joys with each other. While this was not true of all prisoners, some of us banded together and felt fortunate to be able to do so.

Among the hopes that filled our hearts was that—perhaps, perhaps, perhaps—a miracle would happen. Perhaps God would save us. Perhaps we could escape and save ourselves. Perhaps we would be liberated.

To prepare for such a possibility, we met secretly twice a week in groups, or cells, of ten men. Each group had two contact men, each of whom stayed in touch with a contact man from another group. We shared our knowledge and skills with each other. We served as vehicles for the underground to spread news of the outside world. We spread hope.

The system was cleverly devised. The Nazis could not force any of us, even by torture, to reveal the names of more than ten members, because we knew no more than ten. Even the contact man knew only the nine other men in his group and one contact man from another group. In this way, we protected the resistance movement.

The head of our group was my friend, Abram Danziger, who had helped me when I was recovering from the beating I received in Krosniewice. He was proving himself to be a born leader. I was one of the few to know that he was a contact man for another group.

Our group somehow came in contact with partisans on the outside. We learned that even some members of the German *Gestapo* (Nazi police) and the *Wehrmacht* were sympathetic to our cause and were helping us. This gave us a ray of hope.

Abram Danziger pulled me aside one day. He was excited, but noticeably nervous. "Abe, I want you to know something," he said quietly. "We are planning a mass escape. We won't know exactly when the revolt will take place until it is about to happen. On the night of the escape, at about 8:00 P.M., the air raid siren will sound. The Germans will routinely disconnect all electricity to keep any light from giving clues to the bombers that they will think are coming. We will use this opportunity to cut the fence with tin snips that we have already acquired. Four of us will seek out a given guard, attack him, disarm him, and, if necessary, kill him. We will then climb the towers to kill the guards and take their weapons. Many of us will then be able to break through the fence and run for our freedom. We know that Russian partisans [nonmilitary resistance fighters] are about 10 kilometers from us, hiding in the forest. It is our goal to escape and meet up with the partisans." Abram's voice was shaking as he spoke. "I know that I can trust you and depend on you, Abe," he whispered. "I want you to be one of the four to cut the wires and climb the towers."

I could hardly believe it. This is what we had been hoping and praying for. Finally, it seemed that we were going to try to escape. Even if we were killed in the process, at least we would be doing something to thwart the efforts of our oppressors.

"You can count on me!" I said with conviction. "You can count on me."

Our attention in our meetings turned to preparation for the uprising. Each man learned what his particular role would be. Although we had no weapons with which to practice, we had drawings and descriptions of weapons. Although I had never held a grenade in my hand, I learned what a grenade looked like, how it worked, how to throw it, and how to use it most effectively. We would learn where to get these weapons about an hour before the uprising would take place. I looked forward to the day when I could use my new talents to tear open the gates and breathe the free air. We planned to make history in the fall of 1944. I believe it was to be a Tuesday night.

Unfortunately, life and circumstances are unpredictable. Abram told me that the revolt had been planned and delayed several times, but a group of *Sonderkommando* decided that they could wait no longer. One afternoon the Germans had scheduled the extermination of a group of *Sonderkommando*. In order to prevent news of the Nazis' dastardly deeds from ever reaching the outside world, the Germans regularly lured the *Son-*

derkommando by some trick into a place where they could exterminate them en masse. They wanted to leave as few witnesses as possible, and they knew that dead men make poor witnesses. Then the secretly recruited new *Sonderkommando* would take these Jewish bodies and burn them in the crematories.

However, that afternoon, when several soldiers approached the *Sonderkommando* to lure them to their deaths, they began the revolt prematurely. Hundreds of *Sonderkommando* joined in the battle that ensued. They set fire to one of the crematories. Many died in the battle that took place. A few did make it to the sanctuary of the Russian partisans. They had their freedom at last in the forest.[4]

There was a young woman, Rozia, who worked at an ammunition factory and also played a part in the resistance movement. Every day, as we marched to work, we passed the ammunition factory where female prisoners worked. They worked at a fast pace in the overcrowded factory. It was stifling hot inside, so the Nazis allowed the women to keep the doors open. They could walk several yards outside for a breath of air.

Our friend Rozia could not leave her machine, because it needed constant monitoring. Through her helper, Gucia, I was able to exchange notes with Rozia. I often sent her food that I could spare. Rozia looked very much like Ester, whom I missed and loved. She, too, had deep-set black eyes, framed by wavy tresses of shiny, charcoal-colored hair. She lit a fire deep in my heart.

As time passed, I gave in to my feelings of compassion and infatuation for Rozia. Daily as I walked to and from work, I would either risk my life by throwing her a note to say hello or more often would throw her some extra food I had. She would smile at me, and I would consider that a day that the sun was shining for me. I used to tell my friend, Leon Kruger, "When we get out of this place, that's the girl I'm going to marry." I thought about her constantly and often convinced Leon to come with

4. Deciding the *Sonderkommando* unit was no longer needed, the Nazis selected for death 300 of its men on the afternoon of October 7, 1944. Feeling desperate, the *Sonderkommando* unit staged a premature and suicidal escape attempt, killing a few SS guards and setting crematorium #4 on fire. Because it was daylight, those who managed to escape were soon located and captured.

me when I would go to see her. What a shock it was when my friends cornered me and told me, "Abe, you are a fool. Rozia is not in love with you. She is in love with a German *Kapo*."

I could not believe it. My heart, my ego, and my pride hurt. During this hour of bitterness, I sat down and wrote her a letter. I reminded her of how good I had been to her and how much I had risked for her friendship and her love. I expressed my love for her. I again risked my life and threw the note over the fence to her. I was a sad man, a hurt man. Soon I received a reply from Rozia, that read:

Dear Abe,

I'm sorry that you feel the way you do. I didn't mean to mislead you. I never asked you to give me food, and I never told you that I loved you. In truth, I gave my sister much of the food you sent to me. She needs it more than I do. Everyone who works in the ammunition factory has plenty of food. I will always remember that you helped me to save my sister's life. And, yes, it is true. I am in love with a German *Kapo*. We hope to escape and make a life together. Thank you for all of your love and compassion. You are a fine man, and you flatter me with your love. I never meant to hurt you.

Rozia

I still did not really believe it. One day I gathered the courage to speak with the German *Kapo*, with whom I was friendly. I told him my side of the story and asked him about Rozia.

"Abe," he said, "it is true. Rozia and I are in love, and, when circumstances permit, we plan to escape and build a new life together. I love her with all my heart and would do anything to be by her side."

After hearing these words, I understood that he genuinely cared for Rozia. I also understood the plight of Rozia's sister; I, too, would also want to help my sister if she were there by my side. I fully realized that Rozia had never told me that she loved me. As difficult as it was, I accepted the truth and adjusted my life accordingly.

Rozia and her *Kapo* were never to escape and have a life together. After the *Sonderkommando* uprising, the German High Command launched an intensive investigation to determine how they got their weapons and ammunition. The Nazis learned that little Rozia, who worked in the ammunition factory, had supplied the stolen ammunition. Unfortunately it was a Jew, Kapo Schwartz from Czechoslovakia, who was the informer. Few are as mean as Kapo Schwartz, and he played into the hands of the Germans. The Nazis took Rozia from her factory post and put her in jail on the men's side of the camp.

The Nazis wanted to instill fear in us, to teach us that no one could expect to escape, whether they be *Sonderkommandos, Kapos,* or just rank-and-file prisoners. They wanted revenge. The Nazis assembled us at the evening lineup and called out a list of prisoner numbers, as a black flag hung overhead. These designated men remained in their places as the rest of us marched off. The Nazis herded them into separate barracks and executed them the following day. It put a sad, helpless feeling in our hearts.

Poor little Rozia suffered indeed. Later we learned from other Jews in prison with her that she was terribly tortured before she closed her eyes in the relief of death. Rozia had always been an attractive girl, but the Nazis tortured her for three months in the most devious ways. They had men who were specially trained in the art of torture. They burned her nails, pulled her breasts, and tied and yanked her nipples. The Nazis pulled all her hair out of her head and her body, knocked her teeth out of her mouth, and burned parts of her body. After three months of torture, Rozia was still as loyal as on the day they arrested her. She never revealed her contact and never revealed the names of any of the men who collaborated with her in our plans for rebellion.

Rozia faced her executioners like the heroine she was. One evening, as we marched back from work, there was an air of festivity in the camp. A band was playing, and the Germans assembled us around newly built gallows. As was their custom, they forced members of Rozia's family to stand up close, making it more sad for the dying as well as the next of kin, hopelessly witnessing their loved one being killed as the trap swung open.

The drum roll began. Rozia walked out. She was not the same girl I had remembered. Her face was withered, her mouth without teeth was shut. Her legs showed bruises, and despite it all, she held her head high with pride. She walked like the little lady she was and gave her neck to the executioner for hanging.[5]

Author's Note: The hangman himself, Jakob Kozelczuk, was part of the resistance. He was a huge Jewish man, formerly a champion boxer in Poland. He had taken the job of jailer and hangman to help the underground as best he could while inside the camp. He was as kind and gentle as he was large. It was not long before the Germans learned that he was part of the Polish underground, and he was to meet his own death by hanging. His friends, however, cut the rope, and it snapped as he dropped through the trap door. They hoped that the Nazis would observe international law and spare his life, as the end of the war was nearing. The Nazis, however, took him to jail and later shot him to death.

5. Rozia was apparently Roza Robota, arrested on October 10, 1944, along with two other women, fourteen men from the *Sonderkommando*, and other leaders of the revolt. Roza and three other girls were hanged on January 6, 1945, after months of torture. Martin Gilbert, *The Holocaust* (Henry Holt: New York, 1985), p. 747.

Helping Others

T ruth is stranger than fiction," we have said. No one knows
what tomorrow will bring nor what fate lies before him. One
evening in late fall of 1944,[1] after we returned from work, Abram
Danziger ran to me with exciting news. "Guess what!" Abram
exclaimed. "There is a man named Chaim Arnavi on the transport that just arrived, and he may be the man you have been
telling us about."

I could hardly believe it. My heart began beating faster. I thought
of a thousand things I would say to Mr. Arnavi when I greeted him. This miracle that I had prayed for would become a reality. I could now repay him for so much he had done for me.

I had confided in Abram about Chaim Arnavi. "Were it not
for Mr. Arnavi and his warm helping hand, I would not be alive.
How wonderful it would be," I had often said, "if I could only
see the man again to thank him and repay him in some way for
his great goodness to me."

It was the normal operating procedure to quarantine new arrivals
for two weeks to halt the spread of disease, since the disease among
the working force would deprive the German war machine of

---

1. The summer of 1944 saw the destruction of 400,000 Hungarian Jews in May
and June, the invasion of Normandy by Allied forces on June 6 (D-day), and the
liberation of Maidanek death camp by the Russian army on July 24. With the liberation of Maidanek and the steady progress of the Russian army into Poland, the
death marches (the evacuation of camp inmates) back into German-occupied terri-
tories began in July. And, on August 6, the 70,000 Jews left in the Lodz Ghetto
were deported to Auschwitz and gassed.

By late fall 1944, the gassing at Auschwitz had ended, and the destruction of the
gas chambers was ordered by Heinrich Himmler. The last gassing took place on
November 28.

On December 16, 1944, Allied forces began the Battle of the Bulge.

free labor. I could not wait until the quarantine period was over to see if this was the Chaim Arnavi I knew. I managed to sneak into the barracks where I had been told I could find Mr. Arnavi. I looked everywhere, but I could not find him. In desperation I began shouting, "Chaim Arnavi, Chaim Arnavi, are you here?"

From a corner of the room in which I had looked earlier and saw only the remains of men—certainly nothing of Chaim Arnavi—came the weak answer, "Here I am. Who wants me?"

I beheld Chaim Arnavi, but he was not the same man I used to know. I could scarcely believe my eyes. He sat drooped with only a thin layer of skin covering the bones that stuck out all over. He was a living, breathing shadow of a man. His cheeks were drawn. His entire head had shrunk, and his skull showed a deep depression. Mr. Arnavi was dependent upon his eyeglasses to see, and the Germans had broken them to spite him. He looked pitiful and lovable at the same time. I rushed over to him. His quivering arms enfolded me. Several tears wet my neck as we embraced like long-lost friends to whom friendship was all powerful.

With a whispering voice, weakened by thirst, hunger, and weariness, he began telling me of his uninterrupted series of misfortunes. Since we parted, one terrible thing after another had happened to him. Chaim Arnavi was about 37 years old, but he had the frame and looks of a man in his sixties. The Nazis had drained him of life and strength. I was 21 years old, and similar hardships would have weighed far less when placed upon my shoulders.

"I haven't eaten for days," he said to me.

My eyes filled with tears. "Finally, after all these years," I thought, "I can finally repay Mr. Arnavi for all he has done for me." I ran as fast as my feet could carry me, and within minutes I was back at his side. I gave him my entire reserve supply of bread, which I had hidden under my pillow. "Eat," I said. "Eat! I have plenty of food." Mr. Arnavi took two bites but was reluctant to finish, because he thought this was all I had. He did not want to deprive me of it. "Eat," I repeated. "I have plenty of food. Please eat." Little by little, this frail figure of a man somehow found an emptiness in his very being and eventually swallowed a whole loaf of bread. How pleased and proud I was that here I was finally able to return, in some small measure, the kindness and sacrifice that this wonderful man had shown me in years past.

When the quarantine period was over, the Germans assigned Mr. Arnavi to slave labor, unloading bricks and carrying them to a work site. This assignment was sure to kill him in days or less. I tried to move heaven and earth to save him, and luckily our *Kapo* was a friendly man with a good heart. I spoke to him about the plight of my friend.

"I will try to do something for you," he said. "I will speak to his *Kapo* and try to have him transferred to our *Kommando*." Mr. Arnavi soon joined our work crew. This probably saved his life, because he only had to do a minimum of work with us. Mr. Arnavi slowly regained his strength, recuperated, and almost became a shell of a human being.

Dozens of times the thought came to me that I am alive by a miracle, and that I owe so much to my fate, to my Jewish faith, and to my God. I also owed my life to the sacrificial generosity, the friendship, and the helpfulness of Chaim Arnavi.

One morning, our work detail took us to the attic of one of the barracks in the women's camp. Some of the barracks had been damaged by shrapnel from Allied bombing and had to be repaired. Whatever bombing had occurred at Auschwitz, however, it was not enough. We prisoners certainly would have risked being killed by bombs for an opportunity to be saved.

While I was working, a young girl approached me meekly. Her recently shaved head showed a thin crop of blonde hair. She was small and emaciated, but still rather pretty. "Could you help me?" she began. "My name is Zosia. I am from Warsaw. When the Nazis turned part of Warsaw into a ghetto for the Jews, I managed to escape to Hungary. I used forged identification papers showing that I was a Pole, not a Jew, looking for work in Hungary. This worked for a while, but a German officer examined my papers and realized that they were forged. He had me sent here, and they placed me in quarantine. I saw someone I know on the other side of the camp. His name is Mr. Davidson. Please ask him to help me."

"Why don't you ask him yourself?" I answered.

"We are not allowed on the other side of the fence, because we are in quarantine. They treat the women better there. The Nazis use them for experimental purposes.[2] Mr. Davidson is working over there," and she pointed him out to me. "Please," she said, "you have freedom to go from place to place. Please tell him that I am here, and ask him to help me." She pointed him out to me. "He will remember me. All I want is a little food."

Several hours later, I managed to find an excuse to wander over and talk to Mr. Davidson. I faithfully delivered Zosia's message.

"Yes," said Mr. Davidson, "I know her, but I am not going to do anything for her. I have myself to think of. She is on her own, just as I am."

I had the sad duty of taking this empty message back to Zosia. As I spoke these words, her face fell. Looking at the hurt expression on Zosia's face, I felt the terrible disappointment she had to digest. I remembered how I had helped Rozia, only to be hurt in return. "Never again!" I had told myself after that heartbreaking experience, but I decided to make an exception in this case. Coming face to face with another human being wanting food, I could not bring myself to turn away without helping her.

I placed my hands on her shoulders to let her know that she had a friend. Her eyes met mine, and I said, "As long as I am allowed to work in your section, I will bring you food." During the next few weeks, I went out of my way and risked severe punishment to bring food, mostly bread, to Zosia.

Soon, I learned, unbeknown to Zosia, that the Nazis had assigned her the same job that they had originally assigned to Mr. Arnavi, unloading heavy bricks and carrying them from trucks to a building site. I realized that all my help might have been

2. Medical experimentation, an inhumane operation in all camps, was big business at Auschwitz/Birkenau, which had excellent experimental facilities, a massive pool of experimentees, and the growing attention of business, industry, science, and the military. Konnilyn Feig, *Hitler's Death Camps* (New York: Holmes and Meier, 1979), pp. 347-48.

for nothing. This type of work meant that she would soon die of exhaustion. It would have drained life and strength from a strong man, let alone from a weak young girl. I began thinking and meditating on a way to help her.

Again, I called on Kapo Braun. He managed to have Zosia moved from this suicidal assignment to work in the *Kanada*, the Nazi's storehouse for valuables stolen from the prisoners. Her job was to sort the accumulated piles of sweaters, coats, and other items into categories. The work was easy, and she now had a chance to survive. Zosia never knew this and I never met her again, but in my heart I knew I had done something to save a life from certain death.

The Death March

Frightening, but exciting, rumors soon spread throughout the camp. We heard that the Allies were scoring heavily against the Germans in Russia and that the Germans were on the run. The German High Command was consolidating its strength. The Nazis were sending their underlings to the front to fight, while more important members of the military were coming home.

One evening our *Kapo* came to our bunks, dressed in a Nazi SS uniform. Tears streamed from his eyes. "As you know, I am a criminal prisoner," he said. "The German Command forced me from my civilian job and sent me here to be a *Kapo*. Now, they have assigned me to fight at the Russian front. They have told me that I will earn full freedom when I finish my service. They will also wipe my criminal record clean, but I know that many men are dying at the Russian front. I don't know whether to desert or serve my country."

We wished him well and sadly said our good-byes. We also thanked him for everything he had done for us. He had treated us well, while many *Kapos* had acted brutally. And so our Kapo left.

Another *Kapo*, with whom I had been friendly, came by to visit me. "The Germans are now fleeing," he said, "and they cannot move you around. They plan to gas you and cremate you within the next week. It hurts me to tell you this, Abram. I wish you luck. You are a fine man." He continued and looked me straight in the face. I remember to this day; his name was Mr. Sliwak. He said to me, "Listen, Abe, you are wearing a nice, clean shirt. Don't waste such a good shirt and let it be burned up or taken from you by the Nazis. If you are going to die anyhow," and he did not flinch an eye, "why not let me give you an old torn shirt for the new shirt you are wearing?" I could not speak. My mouth was dry, and my head was spinning.

"No!" I said. "This shirt was given to me by a friend of mine. He risked his life to smuggle it out of the *Kanada* for me. I would rather it burn than give it to you. I'll take my chances." I walked away rapidly. This was not the same man who had always been so friendly to me. He had changed. War and death and destruction can bring out the worst in man.

The end of the road was near, and death was dangerously close. It was nearly impossible to sleep that night, yet we slept; we were exhausted. The following day, the Nazis ordered us to assemble. Standing before us, the commandant announced, "There will be a change of routine in the camp. You will all be moved to Birkenau tomorrow morning, and you can no longer work outside the confines of the camp with civilians. You will receive your orders in the morning."

At Birkenau, the Nazis had burned many of the wooden barracks to the ground. We were told that the buildings had to be blown up and the evidence removed. So it was. We saw members of the German demolition squad using air hammers to drill holes at regular intervals into the walls of the concrete crematory buildings. Into these holes they placed wired sticks of dynamite, and at a given signal this entire area was blown sky high and demolished. For two weeks we had to cart off debris in wheelbarrows and cover the area with earth. They used us to conceal evidence of their crimes from the eyes of the Allies and of future generations.

We noticed that the Germans who watched us were no longer young soldiers. In their place, the Germans had brought in their "home guard," known as *Volkssturm*. These German civilians were ordinary, fine people who were drafted into the German army because the war effort was going sour. Their food rations were a little better in quality and quantity than ours. The sights at the camp shocked and pained these men. They were ashamed that their own German people could have sunk so low as to use crematories to burn human beings into nothingness.

The *Volkssturm* had to follow orders, however, for fear of going up the chimneys themselves. Most of them bewailed their fate to us. They feared that the Nazis would leave them for the Russians to find and to blame for these atrocities.

On January 18, 1945,[1] the Nazis called us to assemble for a "very special announcement." Commandant Schwartz addressed us from a raised platform. "My own children," he began, "you know that we care for you, and we do not want you to fall into the hands of the evil Russians. The Russians would kill you immediately. If we win the war, you will have the great honor of serving the Master Race as slaves. You should pray to your God that we Germans will win the war. We must leave this camp very soon to avoid being captured by the Russians. Because you are like our children, I am giving you three hours' notice to prepare to escape with us."

We had three long hours to reminisce, to think, to pray, and to be afraid. As difficult as our existence was at Auschwitz/Birkenau, I knew the ins and outs of life there. I had become reconciled to our conditions and, moreover, could cope with them. I remembered many incidents in which I was able to overcome dangerous situations that threatened my life. What could I do now? We were sad to leave. We were afraid to leave. We knew what we had in Auschwitz, but we were uncertain of what dangers lay ahead.[2] At the same time, we were excited that the war seemed to be ending. Wouldn't we be better off remaining behind? We didn't have a choice. The three hours passed, and we assembled to leave. Only those too ill to travel were left behind.[3]

The Germans in their own methodical way organized us in groups for our long march ahead. We lined up in the customary ranks of five men in a row, twenty deep. Five Germans, with

1. On January 17, 1945, the Russian army conquered Warsaw, placing them about 150 miles from Auschwitz.

2. Abe had been in Auschwitz since April 1943. On January 18, 1945, the last death march fled Auschwitz for the west. At a death camp where the life expectancy was about eight weeks, Abe survived at Auschwitz twenty months.

3. Auschwitz was liberated by the Russian army on January 27, 1945. By late January, then, the Russian army was approximately 150 miles from the camp Gross-Rosen.

Though, from Abe's description, it seems that the march lasted only several days, in fact it lasted about forty-five days; he and other prisoners traveled, on foot, in winter, about 150 miles.

guns drawn, guarded us on each side of the formation. We started out on what would later be known as the "death march."

As always, the commandant and chiefs-of-staff rode up front in half-tracks, or *Panzerwagens*. Next were those officers fortunate enough to obtain a motorcycle or a side car. The rank and file of the German army and the *Volkssturm* trudged their way alongside us and were almost as tired and exhausted as we were. We marched on into the night and slept on the side of the road, still under heavy guard. It was no use to try to escape. We spent the night resting as best we could.

The following day, our forced march led us on a long road and brought us face to face with a wine and liquor factory. The entire area was deserted because civilians had received knowledge of the Russian advance and fled for their lives. The Germans began trying to break down the doors and asked for our help. With their blessing and approval we broke into the factory and opened the vats, and the Germans had a special celebration. Even though they did not get fully drunk, they managed to sing for joy and wobble on their feet. We could not enjoy too much of the liquor. They gave us a little sip, but our weak stomachs could not stand this strong alcohol.

The march wore heavily on our feet, hearts, and bodies. Fed on the rations of watered-down soup and little bits of bread, many prisoners were no longer strong enough to withstand this long hike. Day by day, men dropped dead in their tracks. The Nazis ordered us to drag their bodies to the side of the road. We left a small pile of bodies after each rest stop. They told us that burial crews were following behind, but I know they did not accord these dead human beings a decent burial.

The Germans had placed our supplies in carts that were usually drawn by horses. They forced us to take turns pushing and pulling these carts along the way. When it was my turn to push, under cover of night, I dug my hand under the canvas covering. I felt various articles, and my hand came to rest on some canned goods. I pulled two cans out and carefully placed them under my shirt. I then had to find a way to open the cans. I looked everywhere for an implement to use but could think of no way to open the cans. I thought, I planned, I connived, but nothing could be done. After walking several miles in desperation, I threw the cans away in anger. No one enjoyed the food sealed inside.

As we walked, many thoughts came to our minds. One of the thinking men and leaders was my friend, Abram Danziger. He made his way up toward the center of our group as we walked. He had exchanged places with one man after another to keep the marching formation intact. He talked to several of us about the possibility of escape. Our guards, occupied with their own problems of being tired, watching their step on the road, and bemoaning their own fate, now let us walk at ease. They let us do as we pleased, provided we tried nothing that would endanger security. Danziger felt that this would be the time to try to escape, while we were yet in Poland. We knew the Polish countryside, but would soon be approaching the Czechoslovakian border, where we wouldn't even know the language.

Our plan was as follows: Three of us would rush and attack the guards, and tie them up; we would take their weapons and run to freedom trying to meet up with nearby partisans. We could easily overtake the tired old men guarding us. Many were sympathetic to us as well and probably wouldn't fight much. After recruiting those men among us who could be trusted with such a hazardous task, Abram Danziger moved up to the next group of 100. At a given signal, hundreds of us planned to escape.

We waited for the appropriate moment, but our plan was soon aborted when two men made a run for freedom on their own. They jumped over a small bridge into water and tried to swim to freedom. Their plan had no chance for success. One of the *Volkssturm* guards shot at the escapees. German officers quickly rushed to the scene on motorcycles and riddled the entire area with machine-gun fire. Seconds later, we saw the two bodies floating on the surface of the water. It put a sour, fearful feeling in us, and our plan that had been so beautifully conceived died because of fear.

That night we came to a farm area. The Germans commandeered a farmer's barns for us to sleep in. It was like staying in a luxury hotel to us. We had straw to cushion our bodies, and the walls of the barn kept the cold wind from blowing on us.

As we lay down to sleep, I nudged Abram Danziger and said,

"What a perfect opportunity presents itself here."

"What do you mean?" he said.

"Well," I said, "we could very easily crawl under some of the hay and hide. When the others leave, we could remain behind and then run for freedom. The farmer who owns this barn took special pains to bake bread for us. He would probably help us." So we planned, again, to try to escape.

We postponed our escape once more, however, because the German officers came into the barn very late that night with long, sharp pitchforks. Holding them up to us, they used the psychology of fear and said, "Don't think for a moment that any of you can try to escape by crawling up under the straw and hiding. Before we leave, we will stick the pitchforks into every inch of this straw, and anyone hiding there will suffer a horrible death. Don't try it!"

We awakened the next morning after a wonderful sleep, well rested and in good spirits. We were sorry that we did not go through with our plans, however, because the Nazis didn't probe the hay as promised. They didn't come into our barn at all. We might have escaped had we the courage to hide under the straw. We ate the food the farmer brought us and marched on.

We marched all day. Many more weary prisoners died along the way. If the civilians in the countryside were not aware of the cruelties inflicted on us behind the walls of the camps, surely those who saw this trail of dead bodies were aware of it now.

Our next night's sleep was not to be so restful. At the end of another day of our grueling march, we came to an old, abandoned railroad station. As we prepared to lodge there for the night, a vicious rumor spread that the Nazis would gas us with a poisonous chemical while we slept. We lay awake all night, shivering with cold and fear.

The following morning, we were still alive to see the sun rise. We wondered if the Nazis had started the rumor themselves, just to scare us. We got up as best we could and continued our march.

As we walked, many could not keep up the pace. There were stragglers, as well as fast walkers. The guards did not concern themselves with formation at all anymore. We changed places with each other and talked. I walked ahead and came upon a man whom I knew from Krosniewice, where I had lived for a while after I escaped from Kutno Ghetto. Henry Kleinbaum was a fine man, bigger and stronger than I was, and he was delighted to see me. We reminisced about the past and became friends quickly. We agreed to stick together and help each other. We shared food, and I constantly looked for cigarette butts for him to smoke. It was good to have another friend to team up with to stay alive.

Our overlords fed us off the supply wagons about two times a day. They gave us only one ration of bread each day, and, whenever we were lucky, during the afternoon we would stop and be served hot soup. Otherwise, our meal consisted of this ration of bread, which we had to divide into three parts to make three meals of it. During this entire march, we had no chance to wash and no chance to use any toilet facilities. We had to relieve ourselves wherever and whenever we could. It was all we could do just to survive.

As we walked, we came upon an apple orchard. Others before us had already chewed on most of the apples, but the leftovers were enough to make us very happy. Our hungry mouths bit into them, and we stuffed ourselves with these succulent bits of fruit.

Soon, the German *Volkssturm* confided in us that we were nearing our destination. They felt they could not take much more marching themselves. They were exhausted. Our destination, they told us, was Hirschberg-Riesengeberge. It was an area surrounded by huge mountains in Sudenten-Gau, near the Czechoslovakian border.

More Suffering, More Marching

About 200 of us arrived at Hirschberg in early March 1945. Hirschberg was a subcamp of Gross-Rosen, the Polish camp I was in before being sent to Camp Dretz. Before us loomed a gate to which we had become accustomed, and it led into a barbed-wire enclosure. Armed SS men watched us from the towers above. Snow and ice covered the ground, and we knew we had arrived at another prison camp. Hirschberg was a waystation, where the Nazis would keep us until they could move us to another camp.

We entered the camp, glad to be at another place to rest. A few hand pumps, located in the center of the courtyard, were the only sources of water in the compound. As usual, they deloused us as we entered the camp. We felt like insects ourselves as the Nazis used large hand-pumped spray cans to mist us with disinfectant.

Our guards had assured us that we would have plenty of food when we would arrive at the camp. Now they told us that there was a shortage of food all over Germany. They gave us potatoes in unsalted water for our entire day's rations. This was our only meal each day.

The German guards called out our numbers and assigned us, in groups of fourteen, to various rooms in the barracks. They allocated each person a straw mattress, a blanket, and a bundle of straw for a pillow. It was bitterly cold, and the guards gave us only enough coal to last about two hours. As the cold winds howled through our drafty barracks, we knew we had to do something to keep warm. We pooled our resources, and we all huddled together in one room. When the Germans ordered us to return to our own sleeping quarters, we shivered all night, but we still managed to get some sleep on the two-tier bunks.

The Hirschberg Commandant made a grotesque game out of cleanliness. We had no work to do at this camp, so he ordered us to use our free time to pick the lice off our bodies. As proof that we had done a thorough job, we had to place these lice in a bowl of water. Each day, an SS officer went from barracks to barracks to inspect the contents of the bowls. Woe unto us if our bowl was not filled to the rim with lice.

After several days, we did not have enough lice left on our bodies to fill the bowls. We devised a scheme to beat this game and thwart our oppressors. We gathered the lice from all the barracks and filled two bowls with them. When the inspector came to the first barracks, he found the bowl filled to his satisfaction. While he was inspecting the second barracks, we sent the first bowl to the third barracks. After he left the second barracks, we sent that bowl to the fourth barracks. This scheme worked well and saved us from unknown suffering.

Life was minutely miserable for our German captors. They wanted us to supply them with a little entertainment. Our German overlords ordered us to learn several German marching songs and parade before them in formation. The commandant assigned an SS officer the task of teaching the songs to this conglomeration of sick, hungry, and miserable men. Even though we were all Jewish, we had no common language. We could not even converse well with each other, much less learn German songs. We came from Poland, Italy, Greece, France, Hungary, Czechoslovakia, and Italy. The Jews from Italy and Greece didn't even speak Yiddish, the everyday language of the Jews. What little German we knew helped us to communicate with each other. The commandant, however, demanded a perfect vocal performance. He warned us that punishment would be harsh if we failed to meet the high standards. We certainly tried to learn his songs, and we certainly failed.

Our depraved German overlords even calculated our punishment for their own entertainment. In the middle of winter, with snow almost a foot high, the Nazis ordered us to strip our clothes and march for them, naked, in the biting cold. We marched in our birthday suits to the amusement of our spectator audience, men and women in Nazi uniforms.

The mind is perhaps the greatest feature of the human being, yet under continuous torturous conditions it plays tricks. One's thoughts become careless. I recall thinking about the Birkenau commandant who had urged us to pray for a German victory before we left the camp, so that we would remain alive and at worst serve the Master Race as slaves. I could not bring myself to wish and pray for a German victory. Instead, I found myself looking forward to the taste of the mystery of death.

After several days or weeks—one's mind under continued stress loses the ability to keep accurate track of time—our commandant stood proudly before us at assembly and proclaimed, "Another transport of Jewish prisoners is headed for our camp, escorted by their own commandant and SS guards. I expect you to make me proud. As the commandant arrives, we will call you to assembly again. I want you to show him how disciplined and clean you are. I will select one of you at random to demonstrate the cleanliness of your bodies and clothing. I especially want him to see how free you are from lice. If the selected prisoner is perfectly clean, you will all be rewarded. If he is not clean, you will all be punished."

The new commandant arrived, and they assembled us for the show. They ordered some unfortunate Jew to come forward for inspection. An SS officer approached the prisoner and ordered him to remove his shirt. As soon as they looked inside his shirt, they saw a crawling insect. It was impossible to live in these conditions without lice infestation. They knocked the prisoner to the ground and dragged him like a sack of manure into an adjoining building. We heard his screams as they beat him to death while we stood there in misery. His bleeding, crushed body was carried and thrown in front of us before he was buried.

I stood there, motionless. Tears slid and froze on my face. My mind was far away. I remembered standing and seeing other atrocities when I was in Camp Gross-Rosen. Hazily I recalled the sad, suffering, sorrowful days there. There was only one plus. At Gross-Rosen, we had food with salt. As the saliva trickled in my throat, I could taste in my mind the salty, seasoned soup that would be carried daily in the large metal milk containers. I then thought of how terribly the Hungarian Jews had treated us at Bolkenheim.

Stunned and silent, I opened my eyes and returned to reality. Flashbacks had to stop. I had to think of the present and of tomorrow, sad as it was. The commandant dismissed us to our barracks, satisfied with clubbing an innocent man to death simply for not being able to appear perfect and pure in an imperfect and impure setting. It was hard to lock the memories of this scene out of my mind, but our tired bodies soon fell asleep.

I was glad when I learned of our departure to another camp, but was still fearful of what was to come. The guards gave us bread with jam and raw potatoes for the journey. They allowed us to eat potatoes before we left, as there was no shortage of potatoes. I ate as many as I could and managed to hide about six extra potatoes in a small cloth sack. The guards told us that our food would have to last for three days.

It was now early March as our forced march took us through the cut-out in the mountains around us. With the instructions to hold onto our bread and jelly vibrating in my mind, I proceeded to digest the future danger that would probably confront us during the days ahead. My experience, my fears, and my premonition told my heart that we would see dark, lean days ahead. Ice and snow covered our path. It was difficult to keep our footing on the ups and downs of the road. We had already worn out our shoes, and they did little to protect us from the weather. The cold winds were blowing and penetrating the meager clothing on our backs. We were all weak and exhausted, but still had to continue our march through treacherous conditions. The cold and pain permeated our bodies and souls.

It did not take long for us to become hungry and thirsty. Snow was plentiful, and it provided enough water. Food, however, was scarce. I was glad to have the few potatoes that I had taken with me. I began eating the potatoes first and saved the bread and jam for later. We marched for two days and rested at night in open fields. I still had a reserve of bread and jam on the third morning. Thank God I had the foresight to secure the extra rations and not gorge myself as others had done. Some of my fellow prisoners were now weak and exhausted, from lack of food and from the difficult trudge through the ice, snow, freezing rain, howling wind, and muddy roads in which our feet sank deep. I knew I had to exercise great self-control; I, too, wanted very much to eat my fill, knowing that in my pockets I had slices of bread covered with sweet jam. It was a temptation I had to resist if I wanted to survive. We marched from sunup to sundown. Our SS guards were also exhausted. We slept again in the freezing cold of an open field.

Our group of about forty men still marched in formation the next morning, but our pace continually slowed. We could not very well lift our feet in and out of the deep snow and mud. Many fellow prisoners fell to the ground, unable to carry their own weight. Our guards ordered those who could walk to help those who couldn't. For those of us who managed with our last strength to carry our own selves, the order to intertwine with and carry those who were almost dead weight was nearly an impossible task. Dragging and carrying the others weakened us to the level of the stragglers. More than a dozen of our fellows finally slipped from our grip and fell, never to rise again.

As we walked, we tried to help those we considered our friends first. My tired eyes sought out my friends Abram Danziger and Henry Kleinbaum. We tried to keep our spirit and smiles as an aid to survival and endurance. By looks and smiles and words and winks, we encouraged one another not to give up as we had seen several others do.

Our forced march took us through many small villages. The roar of the motorcycles that carried the lead officer and the trudge of the men brought curious villagers out of their homes into the street to look at these specimens of human beings with pity. The aged SS men who walked alongside us had little more than we. Perhaps they had better clothing and a little more food, but the snow-covered, muddy roads wearied their aged bodies as well.

As we passed a *Wirtshaus* (a small shop selling beer and coffee), one SS guard stopped and ordered a large cup of hot coffee. As the guard was about to tilt the contents into his expectant mouth, an SS officer raced up on his motorcycle. With one swoop the officer hit the bottom of the cup, scalding the guard's face, and rode off without a word. A moment later, he rode back up, got off his motorcycle, and confronted the SS guard who was now wiping his face in disgust and embarrassment. He said out loud, "No wonder the prisoners are not disciplined. They should be looking up to us and respecting us. Just look at your pitiful behavior! Now get back in formation and march with the prisoners!" Satisfied that the SS guard was now completely humiliated, he stepped onto his motorcycle and rode off again.

This aged SS guard became more sympathetic to us. I guess he felt that he had more in common with us now. The SS guard inched over to us and in a soft, pained voice said, "At least you know what is ahead of you. As Nazi guards, we don't know what our troubles will be when the war ends."

Some hours later, word spread that we were nearing a camp where we would stay overnight. Night was falling, and those of us who carried others found our own strength also draining away. Sorrowfully, the tight grip on those we dragged had loosened. Several more of our buddies slipped through our hands and fingers. Stunned, half-crazed, and asleep, our group simply walked over their fallen bodies. No one knew, no one saw, and no one cared—save God above.[1]

The guards who had befriended us urged us on. "Please," they said, "try with all your strength to make it. Don't fall by the wayside like some of your friends. We don't have far to go." At least a third of our group had already died. We summoned our strength, hoping to rest at the nearby camp. The lights told us that shelter, rest, and warmth for our exhausted bodies were near. With a last gush of strength we arrived inside the camp. Having slept outdoors the past few nights, we found the unheated rooms cozy and comfortable. We washed and shared the few towels that we found. We just hoped the Germans would feed us on the morrow.

1. General practice during the death marches was for SS guards to bring up the rear, shooting in the head those who had fallen in the road from exhaustion.

When morning came, we learned that the resident prisoners had eaten the food set aside for us. We were rested, but starved. I still had a little bread that I had been saving. It took the utmost self-control not to eat every bite of it now. I only took a bite, not knowing how much longer it would be before we would have food again.

Soon, we marched to the freight yards adjoining the railroad station. We never saw the sign giving the name of the town. We boarded open freight cars, something like gondolas, with no protection from the weather. We waited for nearly half a day in the cars before they headed out of the yard. We were glad to be moving, but wondered if the future would be more hazardous than the past.

Our train stopped repeatedly, allowing the switching and passing of other trains in front of us. Air raids were frequent, and when the sirens would wail, our train would pull to a halt. We would then start up again later. The falling snow covered us in the open cars. We huddled close together for warmth. As the Allies' planes roared overhead, nearly all the prisoners hoped that a bomb would put them out of their misery.

As we rolled on for our fifth day of travel, with the rhythmic clickety-clack of the rails in our ears, our stomachs were aching for food. They had not given us any food since we left Hirschberg. I had already finished off my stored-up bread three days before. Others in our open car were dying from exposure and hunger.

Our train came to a halt under a bridge. We could hear and see cars and people going by above us. It was early morning and local German workers were on their way to work. As they passed overhead, they saw us in the train below. On one side of the car we had piled the bodies of those who had died, and the living looked half frozen to death. Out of pity, the passersby began throwing food down to us. They caused us more harm than good. These starving prisoners sprung to life, kicking and clawing at each other for a scrap of food. The food was pulled and yanked until not more than two men were able to eat any of it. Fortunately, I stayed away from the confusion and was not among the unlucky innocent who were trampled to death by their own.

Buchenwald and the Last Days

On the sixth day of our treacherous journey, we finally came to a halt. We walked through the gates of Camp Buchenwald, near Weimar, Germany.[1] Walking was extremely painful. My frozen feet were now bare. Most of us had removed our shoes on the train and rubbed each other's feet to restore blood circulation. This helped to prevent gangrene from setting in and possibly killing us. My swollen feet had pus oozing from open wounds, and I could not get my shoes back on.

We came to a halt in formation inside the gates. Buchenwald had a huge expanse of buildings. It was a large camp with prisoners from almost everywhere in Europe. Even though Buchenwald was still under German control, political prisoners were in positions of authority. Most of them were Russian.

A Russian prisoner stood before us and authoritatively called out, "All *Kapos* step forward." The German Reich usually rewarded *Kapos* with extra privileges for their service. Kapo Schwartz proudly stepped forward, awaiting his reward. This was the same Kapo Schwartz who had informed on Rozia and other underground members at Birkenau, causing them to be tortured and murdered by the Nazis. We hated him for that and for many other dastardly deeds.

Kapo Schwartz didn't receive the special treatment that he had expected. Two husky men grabbed him from either side and

1. From Hirschberg to Buchenwald, Abe traveled 200 miles in six days, all of it without any food from the Nazis during the journey.

lifted Kapo Schwartz off his feet. A third man beat him nearly to death while we watched with the satisfaction that comes with sweet revenge—seeing the wicked get their just reward. These Russian prisoners took his motionless body and dunked it into the disinfectant bath. As they stood him up, his face swollen and pale, they hit him once again and said, "This is your reward for being such a good *Kapo*!"

After joyously witnessing this act of justice, it was our turn to walk through the disinfectant bath. My feet burned until I almost screamed. As I stepped out of the bath, I found several torn towels that I used to bandage my feet. They gave us our uniforms and marched us into the barracks. As in Birkenau, the barracks were converted horse stables. Wooden structures, like shelves, lined the walls for us to sleep on. At least we were warm.

Our first meal after six days of starvation was a delicious bowl of soup. My tastebuds knew it was hot but could not recognize the ingredients. For our hungry dried stomachs this was a feast. I purposefully selected a small spoon and ate the soup slowly. When everyone else had finished his ration, I was still eating and felt like a king.

I quickly learned the routine at Buchenwald. Each evening, we received a ration of hot soup. They also gave us a few slices of bread with a little jelly or margarine that we were to keep for the next day's breakfast. Of course, most of the starving prisoners ate their rations immediately.

Several days went by as we recuperated. I had always believed that a man should work to earn his keep. This philosophy probably saved my life many times because the Germans generally treated hardworking prisoners better and fed them better than those who were merely caged and did no work. For economic reasons, those prisoners who were unable to work did not live long. I was relieved, however, that there was no assigned work for us yet, because I was still limping around with a rag over my frozen left foot.

As my foot began to heal, I wanted to work again. We heard through the grapevine that the Germans would be selecting able-bodied men for work at a nearby camp. My friends, Abram Danziger and Henry Kleinbaum, had already been chosen to be shipped out. I reasoned that to remain at Camp Buchenwald as a nonproductive prisoner would soon mean death.

My chance came, and I almost missed it. An SS officer came to inspect us. Because I was still unable to get my shoe over my swollen left foot, he passed me over. I immediately approached the SS officer and explained that I would love to work. "My bandaged foot is only a little problem," I said. "I just have a little frostbite on one toe. There is nothing really wrong with me that would keep me from working." (Actually, my entire foot had frostbite, and I was in much pain.)

I apparently impressed the SS officer with my sincerity, and he looked me over closely. He then told a prisoner to add my identification number, 124157, to the list of prisoners to be transferred. I was overjoyed that my life was saved and I would be joining my friends in the next camp.

The following morning we were on our way, riding in horse-drawn cattle wagons. At least we didn't have to walk. After a day's hobble and shake in the open cattle wagon—the cold winds drove away the cattle stench—we finally approached our destination. They would not tell us the name of the camp, but someone told me that we were close to Ohrdruf, a subcamp of Buchenwald, about 60 kilometers southwest.

The sun had just set, and darkness had fallen when we first saw the entrance to the camp. To enter this camp, we had to go underground. The entire camp facility had been dug underground, and we were to live in tunnels. The old prisoners who had been there for some time ran out and greeted us warmly. Most of them were from Poland and Germany, and not all were Jews. They confided in us that this was a secret underground rocket facility.[2] The prisoners had to fill the German V-rockets with explosive charges. However, they whispered to us that many prisoners had tried to sabotage the warheads by filling the V-rockets with a mixture of sand and explosives. In this way, they had hoped to do their part in bringing the war to a speedy close by hoping the V-rockets would not explode.

2. Twelve kilometers from Ohrdruf, huge underground mountain tunnels housed V-weapons factories. Ten thousand prisoners built the tunnels. Due to the deplorable conditions, only a fraction survived.

A wonderful aroma filled the air as we approached the kitchen for our ration of food. A prisoner was standing beside each kettle of soup, dishing it out to each prisoner. In front of me stood an old childhood friend from my hometown of Lipno, whom I hadn't seen in about six years. It was unbelievable, but it was true. Meyer stopped serving the soup and he ran toward me, as though by miracle we had both been resurrected. We followed European and Polish customs of showing friendship by a hug and embrace. Meyer patted me on the back and said, "Don't worry, Abe. Don't worry. As long as you are here, I will see to it that you have more than enough to eat. You will never go hungry." My eyes and heart danced for joy. I was now in heaven with plenty to eat.

My newfound heaven did not last long. When the German civilian crew chief lined us up the following morning, he studied me disapprovingly. He saw before him a short, emaciated young man with an injured foot covered with rags instead of a shoe. I still could not get my swollen, oversized foot inside a shoe. He shook his head from side to side and said, "No, you cannot work. Your condition will not enable you to do the type of work that must be done here."

My inflated spirit quickly deflated. The next morning, they shipped me out. I never saw my friend, Abram Danziger, again. I later learned that Henry Kleinbaum survived the camp, but Abram died there.

I was really concerned to be grouped with sick prisoners who were unable to work and who were all strangers to me. It was evident that they were in advanced stages of illness from which few, if any, would ever recover. Each transport truck carried thirty people; twenty-nine in our truck were living corpses. Even though I was the healthiest in my transport, I feared catching these diseases myself.

We finally arrived at Camp Ohrdruf late that afternoon. They classified me with the sick and incurable prisoners. The camp leaders ordered us to use an empty building marked "D" as our barracks. Again, they were converted horse stables. There were no windows and no beds. We didn't even have shelves to sleep on as we had at Buchenwald. We slept on dirty straw on the floor, with only one blanket for each person.

The other prisoners with me did not even have the strength or the desire to communicate with each other. They were simply waiting to die. It was a sad and extremely depressing scene to witness. Whenever one of the prisoners died, someone else would take his blanket and any food that he might have. The horrible conditions made us into animals and scavengers. It was a living death.

At my first opportunity, I stopped two Russian prisoners and asked them the reason for the different letters on the barracks. Using a mixture of broken German and elementary Russian, which I understood, one explained that the barracks marked "A" contained healthy prisoners who worked regularly. Barracks B was for prisoners who were able to do regular light work. Barracks C was an infirmary for curable prisoners who could still work after a short period of recuperation. My barracks, marked "D," contained people who were simply waiting to die. They were called *Mussulmänner* (those who had given up the fight for survival). There were several "D" barracks. I knew I had to get out of those barracks.

My opportunity came the next day. An SS officer walked in, and his assistant yelled, *"Achtung."* I was one of the few patients able to stand for this call to attention. "Are there any complaints?" the SS officer asked.

"Yes. If I may speak, I know I am healthy enough to work. I have always worked to earn my bread, and I feel ashamed that I eat bread given to me without earning it."

I impressed the SS officer, and he called over a Hungarian Jewish doctor, also a prisoner, and asked for his opinion.

Without even looking at me, he simply stated, "Many sick and dying prisoners claim to be healthy, but when they are given an opportunity to work, they cannot do it. Then we only have to bring them back here. All they want is a chance to eat more food." My golden opportunity had faded into a mirage.

After several days, the camp command ordered an *Entlausung* (delousing). Lice had infested to such an extent that they needed to delouse us, our clothing, and our sleeping quarters.

It was long overdue. They ordered us to undress for a shower and immersion in disinfectant. They fumigated our barracks. During all this time, we waited outside, naked. It was mid-March and still cold outside, but not freezing cold. The spring grass had already begun sprouting.

Into this scene walked the former commandant of Camp Auschwitz. I recognized him right away, but he knew nothing of my existence. Fortunately, he stopped and asked if there were any complaints.

I grasped at what was possibly the last opportunity to save myself. "Yes, sir," I said. "I have a complaint. I am not sick but suffer only from a minor problem with my left toe. I have been a prisoner for more than five years. While at other camps, including Auschwitz, I was always glad to work to earn my keep. I want to work, and there is nothing wrong with me that would keep me from working."

Later I learned that the Nazis had a formula for judging whether a prisoner could be cured or not. They looked at our buttocks. If there were still any flesh left, there was hope for a cure. If the prisoner had the appearance of a walking skeleton, they judged him incurable.

The commandant looked me over, as well as the other prisoners. Several of us passed the test. He told us to step aside in a group, after which he yelled out, "Who is the doctor in charge of these men?" The same Hungarian Jewish doctor who had previously deemed me incurable without even looking at me, now came forward. In the doctor's presence, the commandant asked me, "Were you ever examined by a doctor?"

"No, sir," I replied.

"You were never examined, even when you entered this camp?" he asked.

Again I replied, "No, sir, I was not."

The doctor now reaped his reward. The commandant tore off the arm band designating him as a physician and ordered him to empty the outdoor latrines. Perhaps this punishment was not enough for his laziness, which sent many curable prisoners to their deaths. At least he was punished, and now several of us had a chance to survive.

The sun of hope shone for me. They sent us to the barracks marked "C," for curable patients. What a contrast! An attendant gave us a hospital gown to wear. There were clean beds and even pillows for our use. I felt purified. I felt new hope. The men here were sick, but they weren't dying. They were talkative. We communicated with each other.

I received attention from an attendant who wore a Red Cross insignia. He was also a prisoner and not really in the Red Cross at all, but he had some first-aid skills. He unwrapped the dirty rags on my foot. After washing my wounds with peroxide and cotton pads, he placed a dry, sterile bandage on my foot. Twice daily, I had the unexpected luxury of a brand new bandage with medication. It seemed that my prayers had been answered and that somebody considered me worthy to live. I was on the road to a full recovery.

One morning in late March 1945, the first-aid attendant came in with an urgent look on his face. "*Przyjaciele!*" he called out. It was the Polish word for "friends." In all his associations with us, we came to look upon one another as friends. His announcement was tense and frightening. "The American Army is only 15 kilometers away.[3] We are evacuating, but only those who are healthy and have no fever can go. The Germans will shoot all those left behind. They don't want anyone left to condemn them. I will take your temperature."

The fear of showing a fever almost gave me one. The thermometer was in my mouth, and I was ready for the verdict, whatever it would be. The attendant looked at the thermometer, and a smile spread on his face. "You have no fever, Abe. You are coming with us." It did not take long to evacuate the entire camp. We began our long hike back to Buchenwald.

We later learned that the Nazis ignited dynamite they had previously placed at Ohrdruf. The entire camp and all those left behind—the sickly, the stragglers—had been blown into nothingness

3. Ohrdruf was liberated by the American army on April 4, 1945. When General Eisenhower visited the camp, he was so shocked at the sight of the emaciated corpses that he ordered photographers to the camp and had copies of the photographs sent to Churchill. Churchill arranged, at once, for several members of Parliament to visit the camp.

and dust. Some had tried to escape the burning wreckage and debris, but none survived.

After walking quite a distance, they let me ride in a horse-drawn wagon with other sick prisoners healthy enough to keep alive. It was a long, tiring, shaky trip. After a night's journey, we arrived back at Buchenwald camp.

The physical facilities at Buchenwald had not changed, but the German efficiency, previously so evident, was now gone. The guards ordered us off the wagon and into one of the converted horse stables. Three-tiered shelves lined the walls. Some dirty, smelly straw was all we had to cushion our bodies. We simply fell down limp on the shelves to rest.

By now, my infected foot had swelled again. I would limp outside the barracks just long enough and far enough to obtain my food. In my exhausted and sickly state, I would then limp back to rest on the shelves. Almost all hope had left us. We were waiting for the inevitable—death—which we felt would overtake us very soon.

One afternoon as I walked outside my barracks, I saw the face of Kapo Schwartz, the same Schwartz who had been badly beaten when we first entered Buchenwald. He had been beaten to death this time and, for the ultimate degradation, was thrown into a horse trough. I later learned that two Russian prisoners, whom Schwartz had previously beaten and tortured at Auschwitz, had found him in a dark alley and taken their revenge on him. The sight of this dead, ugly *Kapo*—a Jewish prisoner himself who chose an extra piece of bread in return for hating and beating and abusing his fellow man—helped to renew my faith in some sort of justice.

That great power which turns the events of man and nations was now to move in a giant step. . . .

In the first days of April 1945, word began to filter in through the underground resistance that the American army was approaching. Most of the underground members at Buchenwald were Russians. The word was that the Americans would reach our camp in a few days. Hope again lifted our spirits.

We learned that the Germans were planning to evacuate the camp before the Americans would arrive, as they had at other camps. They would order all Jewish prisoners to march out with them. The Nazis would then use us as hostages, or simply as bull's-eyes for target practice. The underground warned us not to leave with the Germans if we wanted to live.

All these long years, we had obeyed German orders without question, like robots. This order many of us did not obey. We had nothing to lose but our lives, and we wanted to stay alive. We tried to make things difficult for the Nazis; we did whatever we could to resist them.

We had to make ourselves indistinguishable from non-Jewish prisoners, who would be left at the camp. The Germans at Buchenwald could easily identify us as Jews by the red and yellow Star of David patches sewn on our uniforms. Underground members instructed us to tear off the patches. Non-Jewish prisoners helped us in this process by tearing off their own patches. With all patches removed, the Nazis could not distinguish Jews from non-Jews by our uniforms alone. If the Germans had more time, they could have identified us in other ways, such as the tattoos on our arms.

The Nazis rushed around in a state of chaos when evacuations finally began. Almost all the Nazis and thousands of Jewish prisoners had evacuated the camp by the second week of April.[4] I was able to stay behind. Our plan had worked, but I was still doubtful that liberation would come.

During my entire time at Buchenwald, we hoped and prayed that the Americans would liberate us. We discussed it endlessly and pictured it in our minds as though it had already happened. We talked for hours on end about what we would do when that day would come.

We could tell that the fighting was getting closer. Bombs exploded closer and closer to the camp. We heard cannon blasts and the sound of exploding shrapnel. Allied aircraft flew overhead dropping lighted flares. Soon it seemed that the explosions were just outside the barracks. Even so, we just lay there. Even the threat of exploding bombs was not nearly as bad as what we had all been through.

---

4. On April 8, 1945, many Jewish prisoners at Buchenwald were marched out, leaving the non-Jewish prisoners to wait for liberation by American forces.

Liberation and Recuperation

On the afternoon of April 11, 1945,[1] I was resting in my barracks. My body was extremely weak from fighting off my foot infection without nourishment or medical attention. I heard something that I couldn't quite believe. I raised my head to listen. Was it my imagination? Was I losing my mind? I heard singing. The singing became louder and more distinct.

The huge barracks stable door now swung open. I finally believed my ears because my eyes saw a sight I shall never forget. I beheld a miracle. Some of the same German SS officers whom we had taken orders from but moments before, now marched into our barracks with their hands and bodies bound with rope. Some of my fellow prisoners were pricking them and goading them with the officers' own rifles and bayonets. They shouted to the Nazi officers, "Aren't you proud of your accomplishments?" as they pointed to the half-dead bodies that lay on the wooden shelves in our barracks.

Fear replaced German pride and authority. With this wonderful turn of events, we saw German SS officers cringing before former Jewish prisoners. They must have asked them-

1. On April 11, 1945, the American army broke through the Buchenwald gates and quickly ended resistance from the SS guards. Elie Wiesel, fellow prisoner with Abe at Buchenwald, wrote of his liberation as being "the most moving moment of my life. . . . I will always remember with love a big black soldier. He was crying like a child—tears of all the pain in the world and all the rage. Everyone who was there that day will forever feel a sentiment of gratitude to the American soldiers who liberated us." Elie Wiesel, "Facing Hate," Public Affairs Television, November 27, 1991.

selves, "What will the future bring for us now?"

Behind the singing prisoners came the American soldiers. It was unbelievable, but it was true. We had done everything in our power to stay alive long enough to see this miracle come about, despite so many designed traps to annihilate us. We were finally seeing the miracle happen.

The American soldiers stood there like giants, in their net-covered helmets and camouflage uniforms. Seeing them look upon us with heart and feelings turned the clock back to my childhood—I was human again. They assured us that everything would be all right.

We had had to keep stiff upper lips and dry eyes through many years of persecution, of being pushed around, of hunger and deprivation beyond description, of whippings and psychological torture, of being treated worse than animals. We had learned to shut down our emotions and our pain, to turn off our tears. We had ceased to be human. We now began to feel again, to react again, to be human again. We had been resurrected—brought back from a life worse than death—and our American heroes were there before our eyes. All I could do was cry and cry and cry, and I was not alone. Prisoners and soldiers cried together.

The sight of our liberators was too good to believe. We had to be convinced. We constantly reminded each other that it was real. Voices blared continually over the loudspeakers, assuring us that there was no longer anything to fear. The same loudspeakers that had for years carried voices of hate, now sent messages of freedom and hope.

Yet, the human mind plays tricks. Many of us still could not really, really believe that we were free. We still feared that the Germans would mount their forces and take over again. Then they would certainly slaughter us all. These gnawing thoughts ran through our minds, and we discussed them many times. But now all I could think about—my head was spinning with joy at the sight of real flesh-and-blood American soldiers. I had never in my life seen an American soldier; but now these men tore down the walls of Jericho, and the promised land of freedom was opened a crack before us. Besides the sight of the Americans, the scene of our fellow prisoners pointing bayonets against the German

SS officers gave us good reason to smile, to laugh, to rejoice, and to hope.

The American soldiers had their own problems to overcome. They had heard of concentration camps but had never really believed all the stories. They had not prepared themselves for what they saw. It was worse than they had ever imagined. The sight of the living as dead skeletons, men so emaciated that only a paper-thin layer of skin covered their shrunken skulls and skeletons, was a sight too weird and strong for them to withstand. Malnutrition had caused our stomachs to swell. Piles of ashes lay near the crematories, with bone fragments jutting out. Dead bodies were stacked up like cordwood. The stench that we had gotten somewhat accustomed to was unbearable for them.

Many of the American soldiers fainted and fell at the sight. Many more broke down and cried and vomited. Others couldn't help but look away, and I couldn't blame them. We, the prisoners, had become accustomed to the sight of remnants of human beings dragging themselves as though half alive. In retrospect, it was a chilling, frightening, shocking sight. It shocked all who had a heart—all who were still human beings.

Some of the Americans threw candy bars and cigarettes to us. One young soldier had just gained composure after vomiting. I saw the grief in his tear-filled eyes. He began handing out army ration chocolate bars to several prisoners, and I rushed up to get one for myself. I saw him turn around and talk with an army medic. Immediately, he turned and began taking back our candy bars! We fought as hard as we could to keep our gifts, but he finally took my candy back and others' as well. He was saying something to us in English, but we didn't understand.

Within a few hours, the Americans served us a rich, meaty, nourishing soup. Our digestive systems had shut down after years of suffering and starvation, so we could not handle very much of this rich food. Many prisoners gorged themselves, only to end up with severe diarrhea and pain. Some died as a result of eating too much rich food too soon. Freedom and food came too quickly for them, and their weak bodies were not ready. I was among the fortunate few who were able to hold down this feast prepared by the Americans. I slowly ate my fill, but not my over-fill, and I did not suffer like many others. I finally understood why the young soldier had taken our candy bars away from us. The rich chocolate would have been a shock to our malnourished bodies.

This joyous experience of liberation would not have been ours had a little miracle not happened. We later learned, on good authority, that the German High Command had prepared for this overrun of the camp by the American army. They had a contingency plan. When German intelligence at Weimar would receive news that the Americans were approaching, they were to telephone Buchenwald. This was to be the signal to evacuate the remaining Nazis and take several valuable war prisoners with them. The Nazis had wired the camp with dynamite, and they planned to destroy the camp as they left, killing all the remaining prisoners inside. This way they would leave no witnesses and would destroy the evidence of their crimes.

Somehow, American intelligence learned of this contingency plan. The American army wisely chose to bypass the city of Weimar, and they attacked Buchenwald first. The element of surprise helped the Americans. They blasted the walls and the gates. Some of the prisoners overtook the few guards and officers that were still at the camp. These prisoners virtually liberated themselves at 3:15 in the afternoon.

At 6:00 P.M., the phone did ring at Camp Buchenwald. It was Weimar calling. On schedule. The man who answered the phone in faultless German was a German Jew, now liberated. He answered, *"Jawohl"* (Yes sir), when the Nazis in Weimar gave the order to blast the camp. They didn't know that the dynamite charges had already been disconnected and that we were in control.

After they liberated us, the Americans made their trek into Weimar. Their arrival was a miracle that saved our lives and thwarted the murderous plot of the Germans. The Nazis had planned without pity to annihilate every soul—close to 30,000 human beings—who, for no fault of their own, for no crime or sin, were methodically herded and rounded up from loving homes, families living in peace, and made almost overnight into chattel of the Germans. To do with as they pleased. And it now pleased the Germans to blow us en masse into nothingness so as to have the dust and dirt cover our bodies and their evil history and deeds.

Life was quite different at Buchenwald after Liberation. We stayed in the same camp. We slept in the same barracks, on the same wooden shelves. We breathed the same air through the same nostrils, but it was now the fresh air of freedom and of hope. The gates of our camp were still guarded, but by our fellow prisoners to protect us. The gates were always open. We could come and go as we pleased. We felt dignified again.

None but the imprisoned and the oppressed can fully appreciate the meaning of the word "freedom." It is the most precious gift of life. Liberty and freedom are both words that glide easily off the tongue, but freedom arrives through much hardship and pain for those without it. What is freedom? It is incomprehensible. It would take a lifetime to fully express it.

The Americans wanted the local civilians to see how the Nazis had taken this wonderful freedom from us at Buchenwald. They couldn't believe that the people of Weimar, the cultural center of Germany, didn't know what was happening behind the gates. "How in God's name could human beings so torture and mistreat others?" the Americans asked repeatedly.

On April 13,[2] two days after we were freed from oppression, from hunger, from fear, the American army brought in citizens of Weimar to see for themselves what their leaders had done. They brought in the *Bürgermeister* (mayor), other office holders, and many leading citizens. They also brought in ordinary civilians. The Americans forced them to walk through the barracks and see the emaciated, dying people inside. They forced them to see the crematories and the piles of human ashes. They forced them to witness the stacks of dead bodies of men,

2. On April 13, 1945, the Russian army captured the Germany city of Vienna.

Two days later, on April 15, the British army liberated the concentration camp Bergen-Belsen. They found evidence of mass murder on an even larger scale than reports suggested. Photographs, films, and articles about Bergen-Belsen circulated widely by the end of April, making so great an impact that the word "Belsen" was to become synonymous with "inhumanity."

Also on this day, a death march with more than 50,000 prisoners left the camp Ravensbruck in northern Germany for Sachsenhausen. Even though the end of the war was clearly near, Nazis continued to kill Jews under their control.

women, and children, decaying in the open air. The sights horrified most of them, but a few showed no emotions at all. They all maintained that they knew little or nothing about these terrible crimes.[3]

Looking back and trying to place myself in the shoes of these citizens of Weimar, I can now better understand their reaction. There was a look of embarrassment and dismay on all but a few faces. Many of the men and women fainted in horror at the sights and the stench. Several had tears rolling off their cheeks, which they did not wipe away. No doubt these visitors have not slept well since this traumatic experience.

It became evident to me, after I tried to answer unanswerable questions, that many German citizens were truthfully unaware of the daily torture and death practiced in their backyards. The atmosphere in Germany was so oppressive that ordinary citizens were afraid to discuss the politics of the day. Parents were afraid to talk about it in front of their children, and children were reluctant to share their feelings with their parents. If they did speak out, the Gestapo might have rounded them up and placed them in the camps, too. Fear, fear, fear! Everybody was afraid of everybody else, so multitudes of German citizens knew only fragmentary information about the concentration camps.

The German officers at Buchenwald had trained young boys, from 11 to 15 years old, to be *Kalifakter*, or errand boys. The Nazis had forced them to run around the camp at their whim and had treated many of them brutally. The Americans liberated about 100 of these boys. They became kids again. Some of these boys supplied a type of entertainment that was good medicine for us.

For over a week, at about 5:00 P.M. each day, we would assemble outside the jail where some Nazi officers were held. Former prisoners, who were now in control of the jail, would open the cell doors. They would bring out one Nazi officer at a time. One of the boys would have a whip and would order the Nazi to bow

---

3. The army brought German civilians by the hundreds from Weimar and forced them to work in the kitchens, to clean the barracks, and to dig mass graves on the mountainside.

to the ground, or to perform some other meaningless task. If the officer did not obey fast enough—and it was never fast enough—the boy would whack him a couple of times with the whip. One little boy, who but a week before was at the mercy of this particular Nazi, now threw a piece of bread on the ground and ordered the officer to pick it up. No matter how quickly he responded, the boy would find an excuse to whip him once or twice. We howled in delight. How wonderful it was to see the roles reversed. It was vengeful entertainment that was good for our morale and our mental health.

The Americans had arranged to care for the ill and injured prisoners. Many diseases befell the undernourished and tortured prisoners. It was almost natural to be sick in such an environment and a miracle to remain healthy. My foot had become extremely infected. Two husky, well-groomed American soldiers tenderly lifted me up and placed me on a stretcher. I felt humble and small in their presence. They took us by ambulance to the army hospital located nearby. Formerly, only Nazi soldiers used the hospital. Now we took priority for medical attention and recuperation.[4]

The medical personnel gently washed us and gave us clean bed clothes. They placed us on beds with white sheets and pillow cases—a luxury that we had not seen for more than five years. I again felt that I was part of the human race. I felt that I counted, that I mattered, that I was somebody again.

Soon, they carried me into the examination room where several doctors examined me. Of course, I was malnourished and weak, but my real problem was my left foot. When the doctors uncovered my foot, they saw that the instep, the ankle, and

4. As Abe began his recuperation at a nearby army hospital, Allied forces pressed deeper into Germany where on April 25, 1945, American and Russian forces met in the city of Torgau, essentially cutting Germany in half. On April 27, 1,000 Jewish prisoners on a death march from Rehmsdorf to Theresienstadt were machine-gunned at the train station at Marienbad. On April 29, the American army liberated the camp Dachau. The next day, April 30, Hitler committed suicide at his bunker in Berlin, and Soviet forces liberated the camp Ravensbruck. The last of the death marches began on May 1 as prisoners were marched out of the camp Mauthausen east toward Gunskirchen. Both camps were liberated by the American army on May 5, but not before thousands died during the march. And, finally, on May 8, 1945, the German army surrendered to the Allies.

the sole were as black as coal. I had gangrene from the lack of blood flow caused by the frostbite. My foot needed immediate medical attention.

The doctors, former prisoners themselves, conferred on the remedial steps to take. My heart sank when I heard one of them say, "I am afraid that we will have to amputate the lower part of his foot."

"I'm not so sure," I was relieved to hear another doctor say. "He is a young man, and, other than the problem with his foot, he seems reasonably healthy. Let's try all that we can before we amputate. Let's give him a chance to heal." So it was.

Several times a day, the doctors came to cut away the dead skin and apply medication. The nurses changed my bandages regularly. They gave me injections of antibiotics twice each day. These voluptuous nurses brought good food and juices to my bed. Such good care and tenderness, especially the contact with the female nurses, almost assured my recovery. I had not been so close to women in several years, and my sexual desires were rekindled.

Little by little, day by day, I could see my foot returning to a normal color. What had appeared to be a hopeless, black chunk of flesh had now healed through the skillful hands of the capable physicians and nurses. Other than losing part of one toe, I had a miraculous recovery. I could now walk with both feet on the ground. It took over a month for nature, with the help of the Almighty, to restore my foot to health and me to life.

When I was able to walk, I ventured out to the rest of the hospital to see if I knew anyone there. The first person I recognized was Simek Kirstein. I had known Simek since the beginning of the war at Kutno Ghetto. We were also on the same *Kommando* for a while at Auschwitz. We hugged each other joyously. We were so happy to see each other alive. Simek and I walked around, looking for someone else we knew.

It surprised me to find another friend in the hospital, Leon Kruger. I had met Leon at Auschwitz, but had no idea that he was at Buchenwald. I introduced Leon to Simek, and then asked, "How did you get here, Leon? I haven't seen you since

Auschwitz. I thought you were dead."

"I ended up here, too, after we left Auschwitz," Leon told us. "I was sick with typhus at Buchenwald. I couldn't leave my barracks for weeks. I was so sick! When the Nazis called all the Jews to get ready to leave, I refused to go. I was hiding in the barracks when a guard came up and ordered me to leave. I refused, and he hit me on the head with his rifle. All I remember was falling into a deep, sweet sleep. I must have been in a coma, because I slept for more than two weeks. When I woke up here, in the hospital, I didn't even know that we were liberated!" It was good to see my old friend. Simek and I visited Leon every day.

Soon we were able to go on extended walks. We found that the gates of Buchenwald were but twenty minutes away. We walked inside as free men, curious about what was happening now.

We wandered around the camp and soon came face to face with another friend, Joseph Grosnacht. Joe and I had met at Buchenwald. We soon saw several more friends. Because they suffered no major physical impairment, the Americans never took them to the hospital. They stayed at Buchenwald as free men. The food was plentiful and delicious, but otherwise their lot had not improved much. They wore a smile, but there was a sense of hopelessness and concern for the future written on many of their faces. They had no idea how to begin their new lives.

Very soon our conversation turned to women. When one has enough to eat, one naturally thinks of the opposite sex. Someone told us that a liberated transport of Jewish women occupied several barracks nearby. Our feet rapidly carried us there. What a surprise to see another old friend from Auschwitz, Gucia. She worked at the ammunition factory with Rozia and had acted as our liaison for a while, as Rozia and I exchanged notes of friendship. Gucia and I embraced and kissed like the long lost friends we were. Tears of joy and lumps in our throats came but moments later, with prayers on our lips.

Gucia told me about Zosia, the young girl I had helped in the women's camp at Birkenau. I had given her food and other necessities at Birkenau and had arranged easier work for her so that she could remain alive. "You know," Gucia said, "Zosia was here, but she left when she found out that you were here. She was afraid that you would demand your reward for helping her so lavishly."

It was interesting to see how our concerns had changed after we were free. Before Liberation, our most important thought was how to get a little bread to eat or a little extra soup. Now, Zosia worried that I would expect some kind of payback for helping her. Certainly I wouldn't.

A big treat was in store for us. We learned that those aged 21 or younger could register to go to Switzerland for rest and recuperation. After we would spend some time there, we could then take up a trade, emigrate to various countries, or return to Germany. The decision was ours to make. This came as quite a surprise to us. The Nazis had not allowed us to make any decisions about our future since the war had begun. It made us feel important to be in control of our own destiny again. Just the thought sent feelings of elation through our souls.

I decided to go to Switzerland along with Simek, Leon, Joe, Gucia, and several other friends. There was talk about going to Palestine (Israel) after that. The future looked bright. Switzerland was enticing. Our new lives filled with happiness and exciting prospects for the future. After registration, some American soldiers took us to the railroad station, and we boarded a passenger train for Switzerland.

Upon boarding, my eyes almost popped out of my head at the sight of the luxurious train. We had ridden in so many cattle cars in the past few years. Now we were to ride in luxury, and we didn't even have to pay. The joy we had, just to be able to ride a passenger train as ordinary citizens, was indescribable.

Joe Grosnacht, Gucia, and I occupied a compartment together. Many thoughts flooded our minds as we looked at each other. I knew that Gucia had hoped to be with me, while Joe had his eyes set on her. This triangle would prove only to separate us. Each of us waited for the other to make a move.

The time soon came. Gucia, as an ordinary young lady, decided that she must freshen up. She left the compartment and headed for the washroom facilities.

"Joe," I said, "what are we going to do about Gucia? This situation is already beginning to feel uncomfortable."

"I like Gucia very much," Joe told me. "How about you?"

"I'm fairly sure that she likes me," I said, "and I like her, too. She's a nice enough girl, but I really don't care to get involved with her."

We realized that our friendship was too important to let Gucia come between us. We wanted to stick together as we began to rebuild our lives. Joe and I agreed that the solution to this problem was to leave Gucia. We conceived a plan.

Gucia soon returned to our compartment. As soon as the train began pulling out of the station, we excused ourselves and walked out. We jumped off the train together and waved *bon voyage* to dear Gucia through the window as she passed by. We really hoped that she would have an enjoyable life. We were happy to have her go her way and us go ours. Simek and Leon continued on, not knowing that Joe and I had left the train.

Although we had been so excited about going to Switzerland, Joe and I decided to go back to camp. At least it was a place to stay and to get something good to eat. Joe and I discussed our future together. We decided that whatever we would do from that point on, we would do together as brothers.

Upon returning to camp, we learned that Buchenwald was to be in the Russian Zone. The Americans offered us an opportunity to make another decision. We could stay there and eventually go back to Poland, or we could go into the American Zone. We had nothing to go back to in Poland. We both felt sure that the Nazis had murdered our families. We decided to go into the American Zone and take our chances on what life had to offer. We went on our own into the American sector rather than with the American army on their trucks to another camp. We had no desire whatsoever to return to any form of camp life.

Exploring Our New Environment

Soon, a train pulled into the station, and we happily boarded without even having tickets. Joe and I met up with three other ex-prisoners, and we sat together in a compartment. After the train began rolling, a conductor came into our compartment to ask for tickets. Seeing us in prison uniforms, he did not ask us for anything. He just left the compartment and let us ride.

The train stopped after six or seven hours of travel. When we asked why, the conductor told us that they had ended their run for the night. We wouldn't be able to resume travel until morning. The clear skies had darkened during the trip. It was now raining very hard, and we needed a roof over our heads. We needed to wash, and we were hungry again.

The five of us discussed what we would do. It was important to us that we stay within the law, whatever we did. Many other liberated prisoners were vengeful of the Germans. They ravaged the countryside, breaking into houses and taking whatever they wanted. This was not for us.

We were strangers in this area. We did not know anyone, and we had no money for food or lodging. We decided to go to the police station. We could see the lights of a town in the distance, so we began walking. After a thirty-minute walk in the rain, we asked the first person we saw for directions to the police station. We headed that way, hoping to get some food and a place to stay for the night.

We were soaking wet when we entered the station. We discussed our situation with the officer in charge. This German police chief was afraid of us, since we were still in prison uniforms and looked haggard. Wet and tired, we could have made demands, but we made our requests politely.

When we told him what we wanted, the police chief immediately gave us tickets that we could exchange for food and lodging. He also gave us directions to a place to sleep for the night. After a short walk, we reached our destination. We found a large barn set up for male and female German soldiers who were on the run from the Allies. What a change to have prisoners walking the streets as free men and soldiers hiding out!

Once we saw what the barn looked like, we knew we would not stay there. The people were dirty and slept on straw. It reminded us of the camps we had just left. We had no desire to go through that again. We asked for food and ate there before returning to the police station.

When we arrived back at the station, we told the police chief that the lodging place was not for us. We politely requested another location, and he went to his records file. When he returned, he said, "Yes, I have suitable places for you." He sent Joe and me to one place and sent the other three somewhere else.

When we finally located the address, a large, locked gate kept us from entering. We rang the bell, but there was no response. We rang the bell repeatedly before we noticed a light come on in a window on the second floor. A lady looked out for a moment, but immediately slammed the window shut. The sight of two men in prison uniforms, on a dark, rainy night, apparently frightened her.

I looked at Joe and said, "What do we do now? It is getting late, and this is already the second place we have tried. I really don't want to go back to the police station again."

"So let's ring the bell until she will listen to us," Joe said.

We rang the bell for quite a while before the lady opened the window again and yelled out angrily, "What do you want?"

"We just want to get out of the rain and have a place to sleep. The police chief sent us here," I explained. "We have tickets for a night's lodging and we're soaking wet. We don't mean to frighten you. Would you please be so kind as to come down and at least look at our papers?"

The frightened woman came down with her daughter, who ran out in the rain and asked for our papers. We passed the tickets to her through the gate, and she ran back to the house. After the lady was satisfied that we were telling the truth, she sent her daughter back out to open the gate for us. We were extremely happy to get out of the rain.

The landlady gave us clean towels and showed us where the washroom was. After we talked with her for a while, she became more comfortable and friendly with us. "My sons have not returned from the war yet," she said. "You can wear some of their clothes while I wash your clothes and dry them out."

"Thank you very much," we told her sincerely.

We took turns taking hot baths. What a luxury! I never thought that taking a bath was so great before the war, but after years of filth and disinfectant baths, it was heavenly just to soak in the tub. It was a dream come true. I knew that I would never take life's little pleasures for granted again.

We found some clothes to put on, but they didn't fit. They were too big for me and far too small for Joe. Even though Joe had also suffered starvation at the hands of the Nazis, he was still a big man. We were just glad to have clean, dry clothes to put on after our baths.

When we were ready to go to bed, we had another unexpected pleasure waiting for us. Our beds were both covered with *Federdecke*, or feather quilts. I had not seen this type of covering since I left home in September of 1939. The warmth and softness of these comforters, stuffed with goose down, made it seem like we were sleeping in a cloud. We were so glad that we had decided against sleeping in the dirty barn. All the walking and waiting in the rain was worth it. We slept in complete comfort.

In the morning, we were awakened by a gentle knock on the door. "Breakfast is waiting for you," sang our hostess. Wonderful aromas wafted throughout the house. After so many years in concentration camps, the joy I felt being awakened in this manner was indescribable. Waking in the mornings was always so difficult in the camps, knowing that I had to face another day, just like every other day. Now I felt like I was at home again, with my mother waking me up. I missed my mother so. This loving reminder of my mother's tenderness brought tears to my eyes as I curled up in my comfortable bed.

Our clean clothes were waiting for us in the bathroom. After we washed, we went downstairs to the kitchen. We had hot coffee and fresh warm rolls, with homemade butter and jam. An array of cheeses and sliced meats lay before us. This experience would have been beyond our comprehension just a few short weeks earlier.

We sat and talked with our hostess and her daughter for a while. This wonderful woman was in her forties, with warm, motherly charm. Her smile was like my mother's. She wore her slightly graying hair in a little bun. Even though her sons were Nazi soldiers, she didn't look down on us. She told us how sorry she was that we had to go through such horrible treatment. Her daughter was about our age, and quite attractive. She had long, sandy blonde hair that she wore in braids. Her deep, blue eyes made me want to just gaze at her.

We were now warm, dry, clean, and far from hungry. We were ready to venture out into our new world.

We became explorers of a new environment. We ventured out to see the city. It was a good feeling to be able to walk down the streets, unafraid of being seen. We wanted to blend into the civilian population and pick up our lives where we had left off years ago.

We could not, however, simply blend into civilian life. Our striped uniforms boldly identified us as ex-prisoners. The German civilians tried to appear nonchalant, as though they were minding their own business. They couldn't help but to stare at us, however, and it made us feel uncomfortable. Our prison uniforms were shouting reminders of our horrible, painful past. It was now time for us to resume our lives as civilians, but we had to look like civilians first.

It was still very important to us to try to do things in the proper manner. We needed food, clothing, and other things, and we decided to go to the *Bürgermeister*, the mayor of the town. The five of us got back together and tried to make ourselves presentable for our meeting with the mayor. We went to the mayor's office and approached his assistant.

"What do you wish?" the assistant asked with authority, but also with a little fear in his voice.

As the spokesman, I answered, "We are all ex-prisoners, and we want to speak to the mayor about some help to get us started toward a civilian life."

"Wait a moment, and I'll see if the mayor can speak with you," he said nervously. He rose from his elegantly carved and highly polished desk and walked to the mayor's office. This gave us a little time to peruse this plush office. Everything was neat and in its place. There was a beautiful grandfather clock next to some very official looking file cabinets. In our minds, we couldn't help but to compare the squalor of the camps with the luxury of this plush office.

Moments later, the assistant ushered us into the mayor's large, resplendent office. The mayor was a handsome man, and judging from his physical appearance, he hadn't suffered much from the war's bitter days.

He surprised and flattered us with the greeting, "*Grüss Gott* (May God be with you)." In his official capacity, the mayor had greeted us as he would greet dignitaries. All during the war years, Hitler had raised himself to a godlike position of forced reverence, requiring all Germans to use the official greeting, *Heil Hitler*! Now that the war was over, the German civilians had resumed their customary way of greeting one another. "What can I do for you gentlemen?" he continued.

Now I had to find the words to reply properly. "We are all ex-prisoners," I said, "and we would like to return to civilian life. Can you please help us to get some proper clothing?"

I could see the obvious battle that he waged in his mind as we stood in his office. He was the top official of the city. We, in our prison uniforms, were now making a request that no German civilian would dare make. "Yes," he finally replied, "I will help you." The mayor then sat down at his desk and wrote a letter authorizing a local clothing store to furnish us any items of clothing that we might need. The bill for the clothing was to be forwarded to the mayor's office for payment. He also gave us some cash and enough food stamps to last about a week. This was more than we had expected, and we were thrilled. The mayor stood up and extended his hand to us in friendship.

"Thank you very much!" we all said graciously as we shook his hand.

"I am glad to be of assistance," he replied sincerely. "I wish you well." We walked out feeling much better, knowing that we were now on the road to becoming civilians again.

We felt justified in our requests of the mayor, not that we were asking for charity. We were proud people whom the Nazis had robbed of a large portion of life's blessings. Now that freedom had come, we felt emphatically that the Germans owed us at least a little consideration for our many years of deprivation, when death continually stared us in the face. We decided to collect on some of that debt.

We soon found the clothing store that the mayor had given us a voucher for. With smiles on our faces, we walked into the large store filled with shelves and racks of fresh, new clothing. In place of our prison uniforms, we now could choose from a variety of sizes, styles, and colors. Slowly and excitedly, we selected new shoes, new socks, and new underwear. We also picked out new shirts, ties, coats, and hats. We laughed with delight as we looked into the mirror at our transformed images. Who would have ever thought the day would come when we would see ourselves as free men standing upright in new clothing. What a sight to behold!

We walked back to see our landlady. She also laughed wholeheartedly at the sight that her haggard boarders from the night before presented her with now. We stayed with her for the rest of the week. We had only planned to spend one night there, but the hospitality we received convinced us to stay a little longer.

Settling Down

The trains were running and the whistles were blowing, giving us a feeling of wanderlust. We longed to travel. We wanted to see new places and eventually find somewhere to settle down for a while.

All we had to do was go to the station, wait for a train, and board it. We didn't even have to buy tickets, as the trains were just running now, for all to board for free. The train pulled out, heading for Frankfurt. We sat in our new clothes and mingled with the German civilians. We melded into the picture. None of them knew that but a short while before, we had been prisoners of the Nazis.

We soon became friendly with one of the passengers and confided in him that we had been prisoners in concentration camps. He sincerely wanted to help us.

"For you to stay in Frankfurt is not very wise," he said. "There are many Jewish refugees in Frankfurt, and you will not be able to receive the attention you deserve." Continuing in his friendly, helpful manner, he said, "I would strongly suggest that you change trains in Frankfurt, go to Giessen, and continue from there to Wetzlar." We decided to take his advice.

We arrived in Wetzlar and learned that the military governor was a German Jew. He had fled Germany before Hitler's full rise to power. While in the United States, he became an officer in the U.S. Army. They had sent him back to Germany as the appointed military governor of Wetzlar. His name was Neuberger, and he wanted to help us. He was an Orthodox Jew, and he wanted us to live in the orthodox Jewish traditional way.

He bent over backwards to make life easy for us.

Mr. Neuberger arranged for us to stay in a beautiful boathouse, formerly used by Nazi officers. The rooms were large, airy, and comfortable. Mr. Neuberger ordered the housekeeper, Frau Weber, to take good care of us. She cooked for us and kept house, and she made us feel special.

They had arranged for the boathouse to be used by Jewish refugees. Any Jews who came to Wetzlar, needing a place to stay, were sent to the boathouse or one of several other houses that had been set up. Jews would come and go as time passed.

Who walked in one day but Simek Kirstein and Leon Kruger! We never thought that we would see them again, since we jumped off the train that they were headed to Switzerland on. They now had a pretty young girl with them, Ann.

We hugged them excitedly and welcomed them. "You're supposed to be in Switzerland," I exclaimed. "It's so good to see you! How did you get here?"

"On our way to Switzerland," Leon began, "we stopped at Bergen-Belsen, a camp near Hanover, Germany. We met this wonderful girl," he said, as he gestured to Ann. "She wanted to know where we were going. We told her that we were going to Switzerland. She didn't have any family left, and Switzerland sounded good to her. She said she'd like to come with us. Can you imagine this sweet young girl going off with wild guys like us?"

"They didn't seem so wild," Ann said. "They reminded me of my father." We all laughed.

"So after a few days at Bergen-Belsen," Leon continued, "we got on the train again, headed for Switzerland. As we were traveling, someone stole Simek's suitcase. Simek was furious! You should have seen him. He wanted to kill everybody on the train! We just laughed. After all, we had just left Buchenwald. What could he have so important in his suitcase?" We all laughed, including Simek. "Simek then yelled, 'Stop the train!' He pulled the emergency cord and stopped it. Where did he stop the train? Wetzlar! So we got off the train, and here we are."

"And what happened to you?" Simek asked me. "We thought that you and Joe were on the train with us."

Joe and I told them about what had happened with Gucia. We then filled them in on the rest of our story. It was so good to be with our old friends again.

Soon, another Jew joined us, Herschel Menche. Herschel had almost died while imprisoned in Dora, a camp near Buchenwald. The five of us became the best of friends. As soon as Herschel laid his eyes on Ann, he fell in love. Ann was much younger than Herschel, but he soon wanted to marry her. When he started talking about marriage, Ann told him that she was just too young. "So? You'll get older," said Herschel. "What's the big problem?"

The International Refugee Organization (IRO) and the Joint Distribution Committee (JDC) supplied us with ration coupons and food stamps. The average German only received rations of two eggs per week. This was not enough for us to eat.

Mr. Neuberger saw to it that we received eggs and butter in plentiful quantities. He wanted to keep us content, so that we wouldn't want to eat nonkosher food (food that didn't meet orthodox Jewish dietary standards). We, however, were not really orthodox in mind and thought at this time. How could we be, after suffering for so many years in the camps? We wanted to eat everything. Eating only eggs, bread, and butter became monotonous after a while, and we wanted some variety.

It was easy for us to get more food. Eggs and butter were scarce and expensive in Germany, and we had plenty of both. We took these items into town and bartered them for other foods. We brought home an assortment of nonkosher meats and other foods that we had to keep secret from Mr. Neuberger, our benefactor. We didn't want him to find out and lose his trust in us. He was deeply religious and wanted us to be, too. He just didn't understand how difficult it was for us then. How could he? We still believed in God and prayed, but we wanted to experience life fully for a while.

The months passed,[1] and we approached the Jewish New Year, Rosh Hashanah. All the Jews went to the synagogue for services.

1. During the summer months of Abe's stay in Wetzlar, America's war against Japan continued. Following the dropping of atomic bombs on Hiroshima on August 6, 1945, and on Nagasaki on August 9, and the U.S.S.R.'s declaration of war against Japan on August 8, the Japanese surrendered on August 14, 1945.

To show our respect for the holiday, Mr. Neuberger expected us to wear the traditional Jewish head coverings, or *yarmulkes*. On the eve of the Jewish New Year, I found myself without a head covering as Mr. Neuberger was approaching me in his jeep, as I was on my way to the synagogue. I did not want to offend him and would rather he not see me without my head covering. I quickly jumped behind a nearby fruit stand to hide. The ground was soft and muddy from the rain. I slid and broke my elbow. Feeling guilty, I went to synagogue anyway, while my arm swelled in pain. After services, my friends took me to the hospital to have it set.

It was now October 1945.[2] Our boathouse home was great for the summer, but the nights were rather cool as fall approached. There were no heating facilities, so Mr. Neuberger arranged a new home for us, owned and occupied by a former Nazi officer and his family. Mr. Neuberger gave them only a few hours to gather their belongings and leave the house. This certainly made us feel good, recalling how the Nazis had done the same to us.

When we arrived at the house, we noticed that it was picture perfect from any direction. It was a beautiful home with sleeping quarters both upstairs and downstairs. It even had a bedroom in the attic. Joe Grosnacht and I occupied a room on the first floor. The rest of our group took rooms upstairs. We had no shortage of food or clothing. We lived from day to day, eating, sleeping, and doing nothing. We had a maid to do the cooking and the cleaning. This unproductive existence soon became boring to us.

I went to work as an electrician's apprentice at a large firm, Budrus Eisenwerke. The firm produced steel pipe, machinery, and wood-burning stoves. With a means of income, I began paying the housekeeper for her services. I felt that I was earning my own way, without being dependent on anybody else for survival.

Now that I was employed, I treated myself to a bicycle. I rode to and from work each day, proudly waving to the people I passed.

2. Next month (November 20, 1945) would mark the beginning of the Nuremberg Trials, where high-ranking Nazi officials were put on trial for their crimes against humanity. In mid-October 1946 those sentenced to death were hanged.

Survivors created a strong camaraderie after the war. Top to bottom, left to right: Chaim Gisser, Abe, an American soldier, Simek Kirstein, Joe Grosnacht, Leon Kruger, and Meyer Gisser.

Used by Nazi officers during the war, this boathouse was a temporary home for Abe and his friends as they resumed normal life after Liberation.

Abe sought to better himself almost immediately after the war, 1947.

My feeling of self-worth was growing each day.

My boss, Herr Seliger, and I worked together. Herr Seliger was a refugee from East Germany, and he treated me warmly. He realized that my German was not the best, and he helped me to improve my language skills.

My apprenticeship training covered a wide range of duties. From 6:00 A.M. to 2:00 P.M., my job took me throughout the plant to perform all house electrician duties. We also did lineman work outside, climbing power poles. I spent my time well, and each day proved to be a happy one.

Monday through Friday were my regular days for work. Saturdays, Sundays, and evenings were my own. I spent many hours listening to radio programs. Music and news were very important to me, and I listened as often as I could. I also frequented the local movie theaters. When the weather allowed, I rode my bicycle around the wooded area. The fresh air invigorated me. I enjoyed the scenery that surrounded the city of Wetzlar, and I made new acquaintances with each passing day.

The money I earned had little value, since I could not legally buy more than the rationed commodities. Beyond paying for my trips to the theater and paying our housekeeper, the excess money was worthless. I worked for the satisfaction and education that came with the job, and for the little I could acquire on the black market. With a week's wages, I could only buy one carton of cigarettes on the black market. For only two American cigarettes, however, I could get a pound of butter. It was much better to have goods to trade than money that I couldn't even spend.

Many of the recently liberated men were angry. They felt that the world, especially Germany, owed them much. They wanted to take it easy and live off rehabilitation money for a while. Previously, their lives were empty. Now they would fill it with many women, much food, and plenty of excitement. They wanted to make up for lost time!

In contrast to their outlook on life, I was, as always, a quiet, well-mannered man. I did not rant and rave, nor boast and complain. I seriously planned my future. I also wanted to make up for lost time, but in different ways. My emphasis was not on fun and excitement, but on my education and future career. Friends teased me often for working while others were content to live off the rations and comforts supplied to us by the United Nations Relief and Rehabilitation Administration (UNRRA) and other organizations. I let them tease.

God created man as a gregarious being. He loves friendship and the company of others, especially when he is deprived for so long of the social amenities and graces. We were now free, but many of us had not yet adjusted completely to our freedom. We lacked the company of the opposite sex. I wanted companionship—meaningful companionship.

I soon began visiting a Jewish displaced persons' camp. I attended amateur shows and Jewish get-togethers. I enjoyed conversing with others there in Yiddish. Those who managed our program of adjustment tried to bring normalcy to our lives, with a sprinkling of happiness. They organized social evenings and taught dancing lessons twice a week. I learned to dance waltzes, fox trots, and tangos.

I found myself surrounded by many people at these gatherings, yet I still felt uncomfortably alone. I was fearful and somewhat withdrawn, afraid of what the evening might bring. I felt like a teenager going out on his first date, even though I was now 23 years old. I had missed those teenage years of courting young ladies.

On my first such evening, the organizers announced that the men were to line up on one side of the dance hall and the ladies were to line up opposite them. Each man was to select a dancing partner. My eyes eagerly roamed the line of waiting girls. It was difficult for me to choose, yet I had to choose. What shall I look for? How shall I approach her? Am I too short? Is she too tall?

I soon spotted a young girl who was about my height with black hair, a shapely figure, and a radiant smiling face. I gathered all my courage, forced a smile on my face, and walked over to her. Mindful of the proper formalities I had learned, I bowed, introduced myself, and said, "May I have the pleasure of dancing with you?" In the seconds that elapsed, which seemed like an hour, she gave me an affirmative nod. While we were dancing, she introduced herself. Martha Strauss was the first girl I had held in my arms as a free man. What a wonderful feeling!

My heart was pounding furiously, and I could feel the blood coursing through my veins. Certainly she would notice, I thought. We danced together for a while and soon changed partners. Before we left for the evening, I asked Martha for a date. She agreed, but not enthusiastically.

We met for the date and went for a walk. Our conversation led to my past. She told me how sorry she was and assured me that neither she, nor anyone in her family, had any part in the concentration camp experience. I dated Martha several more times, but she never seemed eager to be in my company. I decided that it would be foolish for me to pursue her friendship.

I soon began to think of my future in terms of marriage. I was eager to pursue the friendship of Jewish girls—my parents had taught me these values—but most of the girls at these dances were not Jewish.

Previously I had tried to seek out the company of Jewish girls who were also survivors of concentration camps. These Jewish girls were few in number—three women for every seven men. It seemed that women were not able to survive the ordeals of concentration camp life as well as men. Having been liberated, these women also wanted to lean on a man for security. I obviously had little financial security to offer at the time, and these few Jewish girls did not let themselves be attracted to me.

I soon learned of the arrival of a family from Lipno, my hometown. I was eager to visit them, especially when I heard that their young daughter was with them. I walked into the one room in which they lived. In front of me sat the mother, who looked and behaved like a peasant. The father had previously been a tailor. The girl was not blessed with feminine charms. As I looked her over, I saw legs that reminded me of piano legs, and the rest of her body was noteworthy for what it lacked. I decided that this girl was not for me, and that this family was not my cultural equal.

My family had earned status, dignity, and respect for having been businesspeople. We lived in a home where culture was always evident. We were proud of our heritage and our upbringing. Jews sometimes call this *Yichus*. In Kutno Ghetto, I felt that *Yichus* was unfair and cruel. Now I understood more of its value.

The local *Gasthaus,* or tavern, was a meeting place for young and old alike. We ate, drank, danced, and sang. I really enjoyed the singing sessions. We held hands with each other around a table and swayed our bodies from side to side, singing whatever songs came to our minds. Sometimes we sang and danced to the music of an orchestra. I met people from many walks of life in the *Gasthaus*, and my number of friends in the area grew rapidly.

I brought my friend Leon Kruger to this *Gasthaus*. He was so excited. He looked at all the people and excitedly yelled, "Girls! Girls! Girls!" He particularly noticed a beautiful girl with blonde hair and blue eyes. We could hardly believe it when we learned that she was Jewish! We went over and introduced ourselves and learned her name was Eva. Amazingly, she wasn't in the camps as we had expected, and she had an incredible story.

"I lived with a German Christian family during the war," she said, "pretending to be one of their children. Our family was very close with this family, even when we lived in the ghetto. When the Nazis rounded us up for deportation, our Christian friends were watching from the other side of the street. One of the Nazis noticed that my brother and I both had blonde hair and blue eyes. He stormed over to my mother and yelled, 'Are these your children?'

"'No,' my mother said spontaneously. She was so quick. 'They belong to our friends over there,' as she pointed to our Christian friends.

"'Send them back immediately!' he shouted. 'They have no business over here with you Jews.'

"So my brother and I ran across the street. We never saw our parents again. We heard that they were killed by the Nazis. We lived safely with our friends until after the war."

"You had very brave parents, and you're quite brave yourself," Leon told Eva, and they talked all evening at the *Gasthaus*.

Like Herschel and Ann, Leon fell instantly in love with Eva.

Very soon, they were all talking marriage and wasted no time in arranging the ceremonies. Herschel and Ann married just two weeks before Leon and Eva. Our house was filling up quickly, and I longed for marriage myself.

My quiet ways attracted the attention of a German lady, Frau Feilinger, who worked at a neighboring house as a cook. She liked me for the serious way in which I faced life—working, pursuing my education, and not carousing with the other men.

One day Frau Feilinger approached me with approving eyes and asked, "Abe, would you like to meet a nice young girl? She is my neighbor, and I think you would really like each other."

"Yes," I said politely. "I would love to meet her." I knew that the girl wasn't Jewish, but I didn't want to hurt Frau Feilinger's feelings. Little did I know that this kind woman would bring me face to face with the girl who would end up as my wife and the source of my happiness.

A New Beginning

Providence kept me alive through my years of suffering in the concentration camps. Providence would now bring Ellie Müller into my life.

It was early spring 1946. I had some extra time one morning, so my supervisor sent me on an errand to the bookkeeping office. I could not help but notice the pretty, vivacious girl with golden hair sitting behind a desk. She had beautiful brown eyes and was just a little taller than me. I politely began a conversation with her.

"I'm Abe Korn," I said. "I work here as an electrician. Have you been working here long?"

"No, I just started a few weeks ago," she said. "My name is Ellie Müller. Are you an engineer?"

"No," I said, feeling very comfortable talking with her. I felt unusually sure of myself as we continued our conversation. "I'm an electrician's apprentice under Herr Seliger. I've been working here for about six months. Do you live nearby?"

"Yes, I walk to work every morning. I live on Nauborner Strasse."

"I have a friend who lives on Nauborner Strasse, Frau Feilinger. Do you know her?"

"Yes, of course. She is my neighbor."

My heart skipped a beat or two. Could this be the girl Frau Feilinger had told me about? Was this the blind date I was to have?

"Ellie," I said expectantly, "has Frau Feilinger mentioned recently that she has a friend she wants you to go out with?"

"Yes, she has," she exclaimed.

"That friend is me!" I said happily.

Ellie smiled approvingly and said, "I guess we don't have to worry about meeting each other anymore," and we both laughed.

"Do you have a bicycle?" I asked confidently. "Would you like to go riding soon?"

"Yes. That would be nice," Ellie said. "How about Saturday?"

"Sure," I said, trying not to seem too excited. I felt like jumping up and shouting!

It seemed like weeks until Saturday came. I thought about my date with Ellie day and night. I couldn't concentrate on my duties. When I happened to see her at work, of course, I just smiled nonchalantly and said hello.

Saturday came, and we went for our ride. We pedaled for hours as the scenery rolled by. We stopped several times and talked. I found it so easy to talk with Ellie. Even though I didn't mean to, I found myself talking about my experiences in the camps. Ellie listened attentively and compassionately. I felt something special about this girl, and looked forward to building a relationship with her.

After several dates, Ellie introduced me to her parents, Heinrich and Maria Müller. They were fine people. Ellie had obviously told them about my past. Her parents showed me special attention. They invited me to their home for dinner. I graciously accepted their invitation, and we had a delightful evening together. I soon became a regular visitor at their home.

One night Frau Müller made omelets for dinner. I saw her adding lots of flour to the eggs, as eggs were still scarce. I noticed, however, that when she prepared my omelet, Ellie's mother used extra eggs and no flour. She wanted to make sure that I enjoyed my meal. Ellie's family, including her brother, Günther, always treated me warmly. I enjoyed the special friendship I had with them.

The months passed and my love for Ellie continued to grow. The genuine affection that I felt from her family made me feel at home. Her home was like an oasis in the desert for me, and I took every opportunity to be with Ellie.

As my love for Ellie progressed, my past religious upbringing came into sharp focus. I had been raised in the orthodox Jewish faith, and I had suffered bitterly under the Nazis, just because I was Jewish. Now I found myself falling in love with a non-Jewish German girl. Ellie's family was Lutheran, as were many Germans. These thoughts agitated me for days, and kept me awake at night.

I soon began thinking about marrying Ellie. After all that I had been through, I finally decided that I deserved to be happy, even if it meant marrying someone who was not Jewish. I had tried to date Jewish girls, but they feared the future and were all looking for men who were secure financially. I was confident in my abilities, but would have to start with nothing, whatever I would decide to do in life. Ellie accepted me for what I was, and we loved being together. I decided to talk to her about marriage.

While bicycling one afternoon, we stopped for a while to rest. I summoned my courage and said, "You know, Ellie, our relationship is growing stronger every day. I love you very much and would like to marry you, but I want you to know some things." I could see that she wanted to say something, but I couldn't stop now. "I would want you to accept my religion, and it is very important that we raise our children in the Jewish faith. Also, I have suffered so much at the hands of the Nazis, that Germany would not be the place for me to settle. We would have to leave Germany."

Ellie fired back a reply that pierced my heart. "What are you, crazy?" she yelled. "You must be! First of all, I am never going to leave Germany. Secondly, the man I marry will be tall with blonde hair!"

Her words were like daggers. I knew very well that I could never meet her qualifications. We sat in dead silence. Finally, Ellie spoke up and said coldly, "Why don't we just pedal home?"

Besides this bitter pill I had to swallow, another shock awaited me a couple of days later. I walked up to the Jewish displaced persons camp to visit some friends and saw my picture posted on the gate with a WANTED message underneath it. I looked up and saw someone talking with two policemen and pointing to me. The policemen ran over to me, grabbed me, and dragged me to the camp police station.

I was dumbfounded. They threw me down in a chair, and the police chief walked in with my portrait in his hands. I knew immediately that they had gotten it from my cousin, Hester, who also lived in Wetzlar. She was storing it for me, or so I thought. The police chief demanded, "Is this your picture?"

"Of course it is," I answered. "What is wrong? What have I done?"

"We have a report that you are a German spy, and have been coming here to spy on us! We also understand that you have even given up your Jewish religion, and that you are going to marry a gentile."

Shocked and flabbergasted though I was, I now understood what was happening. Hester was bitterly opposed to my relationship with Ellie, and this was her way of breaking us up. I summoned my thoughts and replied a bit impatiently, "Do you think that after suffering so much at the hands of the Nazis, just because I am Jewish, that I would now give up my religion to spy against my own people? You can certainly learn all you want about me by talking to any of my friends. I will give you their names and addresses. As for the girl I am dating, that is really none of your business, and none of Hester's business either. I know how you heard all this and got my picture. My cousin, Hester, is just angry and is using you to get at me."

The police chief believed me and realized that he had been duped by a fanatical woman. He promptly apologized, gave my portrait to me, and let me go.

All of this craziness was beginning to drive me crazy as well. Now that I was out of the camps, I was surrounded by paranoid people. I knew I had to leave Germany eventually. I needed freedom, where I wasn't constantly reminded of the past. I began hoping to go to America.

My heart was still aching from my conversation with Ellie. She had calmed down since then, and we continued to see each other. I still longed for a life with Ellie as my wife, but refrained from discussing marriage with her.

My job assignment at the factory changed to repairing telephones. I befriended two girls in the office who were telephone operators. After several days of ordinary conversation, one of them asked how I got the scar on my forehead. My past came to life again. I emotionally told them about being at Camp Hardt. I told them how my German foreman, Philip Brandscheid, had hit me with his cane, his symbol of authority. The scar was a constant reminder of his brutality. The girls were appalled and couldn't believe that such things had been going on.

"You know," one of them said, "if you ever want to find this man, I could get his address for you. If it were me, I'd want to find him and see that he got his just reward."

After this, I became obsessed with thoughts of bringing justice to Philip Brandscheid. There can be a fine line between justice and revenge, however, and I must admit that I also had strong feelings of revenge.

I took my friend up on her offer, and she found Brandscheid's address for me. I also asked her to locate Heinrich Sträter, who had helped me so much as my friend and employer while I was at Camp Dretz, near Berlin. She found both addresses for me.

It was good to be in touch with Herr Sträter again. He had done so much for me in past. I sent several letters and packages to him. He lived in the eastern zone, where everyday necessities were even harder to get. I sent him gifts that I had obtained on the black market. He was very appreciative. I was glad to be able to help him.

I told Ellie about Brandscheid. "Ellie," I said, "you know that I would like to go to America one day. No one with a criminal record can go to America. I plan to press charges against Brandscheid for what he did to me, but I also want to confront him face to face. I don't know what might happen during such a confrontation, and I would like you to be there with me. I don't want to do anything that might hurt my chances to go to America."

Ellie understood how I felt and agreed to go with me. The

following weekend, we boarded a train that took us toward the Rhine River Valley, where he lived. I was careful to approach this the right way. I decided to explain myself to the local officials. When we arrived at his hometown, we learned the mayor's address, but he was not at home. We did locate the mayor's assistant.

The assistant mayor invited us into his home. I explained the purpose of our visit and asked him to accompany us to Brandscheid's house.

"If it is Philip Brandscheid that you want me to visit with you, I'm sorry, but the answer is no. He is a low-life scoundrel and doesn't deserve the merit of my company. You can do whatever you want to that bum." He gave me instructions to his house.

When I found Brandscheid's house, I knocked on the door and heard the words, "Come in." Ellie and I walked in, and he greeted me with the customary "*Grüss Gott!*" and said, "Would you please have a seat? I'll be with you in a moment." He was having dinner with his wife and four daughters. Ellie and I sat down and waited.

Sitting in his den, I was struck by the irony of the situation. How could such a hateful man, who brutalized so many innocent human beings, simply come home to a loving family and live his life as though nothing had ever happened? I looked around the room and noticed his cane hanging on the wall. It was the same cane that he had used to beat me, as well as many other prisoners, for no reason at all. Only he knew how many deaths he had caused with that cane he was so proud of.

After the family concluded their dinner, Brandscheid approached us and asked, "How may I help you?"

I could hardly contain myself. I got up and blurted out, "Do you remember me? Do you remember 1941?"

He undoubtedly thought that I was one of his former associates, because he said, "Please sit down, and have a cup of coffee."

"No, thank you!" I said, as my blood was pounding throughout my entire body. "I did not come to socialize with you. Do you remember this?" I asked as I pointed to my scar.

A horribly familiar look returned to his face as he replied arrogantly, "Well, if I did that to you, you must have been lazy,

Jew. You deserved whatever I did to you." His family huddled in the corner in fright. I felt for them. I knew better than to continue this angry exchange. I left his house with the words, "You will hear from me very soon."

I stormed back to the home of the assistant mayor, with Ellie running behind me. I impatiently knocked on his door, and when he answered, I begged, "Please come back with us to Brandscheid's house. I'm afraid that things will get out of hand, and I want you to witness whatever happens."

He finally agreed to accompany us, but when we arrived at the house, Brandscheid was not there. We waited a while, but the assistant mayor said he would have to go back home. He advised us not to miss our train home, and pointed out a scenic path along the Rhine to take back to the train station.

We reluctantly headed back, and the beautiful scenery helped to calm me. After a little while, though, I noted the rear view of Philip Brandscheid. We were walking right behind him! His pacing back and forth for many months had given me an indelible, wicked memory of this man's walk. As we walked faster to catch up with him, Ellie reminded me to stay calm. When I came within reaching distance, my hands flew forth to grab his coat lapels. As I tightened my grip, an old bearded man walking with him ran off in fright.

"Why, you damned, no good dog!" I said. It felt good to call him exactly what he used to call us. "I am going to drag you through the courts until you get what is coming to you." I didn't realize that I was pushing him forcefully while I was yelling at him. Ellie, who was still calm, realized that the situation could get out of control.

"Abe," she called out, "please let him go. Don't risk your chance to go to America by fighting with this worthless animal!" With these words, I pushed him away.

After I let go of Brandscheid, he regained his confidence and arrogantly yelled, "I am not afraid of you or any courts you are going to drag me through. You and your type are lazy and no good. Hitler should have finished the job he started!"

I lost my self-control and growled, "Why should I wait for the courts to take care of you? I can do it right now." I made a move toward him, and he took off running. I ran after him and yelled, "As soon as I catch up with you, I am going to beat you to a pulp and throw you in the Rhine!"

Ellie again yelled, "Stop, Abe! Please stop! He's not worth it." As I ran after him, I realized how satisfying this whole scene was to me. This man, who had sadistically beaten me and many others just a few short years before, was now afraid and running away from me! This realization immediately cooled my vengeful thoughts. I stopped running and started laughing as I caught my breath. I vowed to finish this up in the courts.

I did pursue this case in court at Wiesbaden, Germany. They sentenced him to sixteen months in prison. This may not have been enough punishment for the acts of brutality he had inflicted on so many others, but at least he was justly punished by his own people for this one act of cruelty against me.

In the fall of 1946, I had a surprise visitor in Wetzlar. Samuel Korn, a cousin from Poland, found my name in a Landsberg camp circular. Landsberg was then a displaced persons' camp in Germany. It had once been a prison that even held Adolf Hitler behind its bars. They printed the names of all known survivors to help us find family and friends. Samuel had come to Wetzlar to find me. Indeed, this was a happy reunion, but Sam brought me sad news.

"Abe," he said tearfully, "I'm afraid that your entire family is dead. All the prisoners at Kutno Ghetto were killed in the spring of 1942. Eyewitnesses told me that the ghetto guards forced all the prisoners to disrobe and board the backs of military transport trucks, which had been hermetically sealed. The Nazis started the trucks' engines and carbon monoxide was piped into the back of each vehicle. They gassed them all. Your parents and sisters were still at Kutno, and were killed with the rest of the prisoners. The Nazis took all the bodies to the outskirts of town. They burned and buried them in large open pits."[1]

I finally had absolute knowledge of my family's death, yet I

---

1. All the Jews from Kutno, Krosniewice, and many other nearby cities were deported to Chelmno and gassed between mid-December 1941 and mid-April 1942. Martin Gilbert, *The Holocaust* (New York: Henry Holt, 1985), pp. 318-19.

was horrified to hear the news. Of course, I had suspected for years that my parents and sisters had been killed, but how and when they were killed were unknown to me. I had written them many letters that were never answered. I always tried to hold out hope, but now I hoped no longer. Death does not come easy; no matter how a person dies, it still hurts those who loved them.

Sam was one of the few survivors who went back to Poland after the war. He returned to Krosniewice and managed to get some payment for his family's property. He even received compensation for our property. He used all of this money to pay off the necessary people for him to pass illegally into Germany.

Samuel stayed with me long enough to receive the necessary papers for permanent residence in Israel.

I soon proudly received my certification as an electrician. I had to pass both written and practical exams. The written exam covered various aspects of telephone systems and basic house electricity. In the practical exam, we confronted problems of electrical installation that we would normally encounter within the home. The tests encompassed practically everything I had learned up to that point. I was now considered a skilled electrician, and would receive higher wages at my present job. I could also pursue additional education so that I could hire myself out for private work as a full electrician.

Even though I was proud of my accomplishments, I felt that being a basic electrician would not satisfy me. I wanted to further my education. I brought the subject up on one of my dates with Ellie. I told her that I would like to become an electrical engineer.

"That's quite a goal," she said. "You know that it won't be easy. I'll help you all I can. I'm very proud of you, Abe."

I applied at the engineering school in Giessen, Germany. The entrance requirements were difficult, but I passed all the examinations and was admitted. The engineering school was part of the University of Giessen. I was fortunately able to pay the low tuition fees from my earnings at the factory.

Giessen was a medium-sized city that still showed many scars of the war. It was about 40 kilometers from Wetzlar, and I commuted by train each day. Even though Giessen had little or no industry, it had many schools and hospitals. During World War II, Giessen was a military center.

I went to school there for about two years. My grades were excellent in most of my subjects. My best subjects were algebra and math, but I had some difficulty with drawing. My hands were quite shaky since my camp experiences, and I often had to bring my classwork home with me. With Ellie's help, I passed my technical drawing class. She had a much steadier hand.

I must have impressed Ellie with my ambition. Even though we both loved each other very much, we hadn't talked about marriage in quite a while. She now brought up the subject herself. "Abe," she said, "I know that you would still like to get married. I didn't mean to hurt you when I told you I would never marry you. I still had girlish dreams. I now know we are good for each other. You are a good man, and I would be proud to be your wife. Whether you want to go to America, or anywhere else, I will go with you; I understand your need to leave Germany. And we will raise our children in the Jewish tradition."

I nearly cried with joy. I had hoped and prayed that Ellie would feel this way one day. I wouldn't let myself count on it though, nor did I try to pressure her in any way. I just felt that I should continue to work hard to improve myself and be as good to her as I could. I cherished her and was so glad to know that we would now face the future together.

Ellie talked to her family about our plans. As difficult as it was to know that their daughter would soon leave them, they supported us in every way. They had grown to accept me as one of their own.

Ellie and I talked long and hard about where we would like to go. Even though America was always on the top of the list, it seemed so far away and difficult to reach. In June of 1948, I had an opportunity to go to Norway as a permanent resident. The thought of leaving Germany, even for Norway, brought some happiness to me. I did not want to ignore the opportunity, so I decided to consider moving to Norway.

I told Ellie about the possibility, and we discussed the opportunities such a move might offer. She said, "It looks good to me, and I would agree to go. You go on ahead. After you get set-tled, write me a letter, and I will come over as soon as I can. We will get married there."

The thought of leaving Germany was swimming in my mind. I had some reservations, however, regarding Norway. I learned as much as I could about this country. I learned that Nor-way was a cold country, that its main diet was fish, and its main industry fishing. This did not appeal to me, and we decided against going there after all.

Ellie and I agreed to wait and try our best to go to the United States. Going to the United States was not as simple as it may seem. I researched the process and learned everything I could about emigrating there. My biggest problem was finding a sponsor. I had to find an American citizen who would help me. He would be responsible for me for one year, during which I would be obligated to work for him. Then I would be on my own.

One evening a friend of mine came over for a visit, and the conversation led to my interest in going to America. I told him about my problem of getting a sponsor. "That might not be the problem you think it is, Abe," my friend said. "My sister and her son are coming to visit soon. They have been American cit-izens since 1928. I would be glad to introduce you to them. I recommend that you ask them for advice."

I made it my business to meet them during their visit. Billy Schweitzer was a few years younger than me. His father, William Schweitzer, had built a trunk for them with a false bot-tom. They had filled this secret compartment with American cig-arettes, and had packed all their clothes on top. It reminded me of the tar barrel we used to smuggle stolen goods through the gates of Auschwitz. They had made it through customs with many cartons of cigarettes to trade on the black market. Of course, I was just the person for that job.

The first thing they wanted was some German wine. The Ger-man beer at the time was not good. I was able to get five bot-tles of wine for just one pack of cigarettes. Billy had spotted a small brass figurine in town that he really wanted, but it was very expensive. I told him that I could get it for him for a few of the cigarettes. I disappeared for a while and returned with the figurine. I really impressed Billy and his mother with my ability to barter on the black market.

The Schweitzers stayed in Germany for several months, and Billy and I became good friends. One day I told him about my wish to go to America. I asked if he would consider sponsoring me. He was surprised and had no idea of how to go about it. I assured him that I had done all the research, and I explained how it would work. He said he couldn't sponsor me himself, but his parents probably could.

We talked to Mrs. Schweitzer, and she promised to discuss it with her husband. "My husband has a glass shop in Augusta, Georgia. He could probably use some help in his work. I will let you know what we can do."

Before they left, I gave Billy two Leica camera lenses that I had obtained on the black market. Leica made some of the world's best lenses, and they were based in Wetzlar. I asked him to take them back to America for me and sell them. If he would then send the money back to me, it would help me in preparation for my trip to America.

After Mrs. Schweitzer left, I almost forgot about the whole discussion, believing nothing would materialize. About three months later, however, I received a letter from Mrs. Schweitzer. Her husband was working on the papers, she said, and I would hear from the emigration office at the American Consulate of Germany. Billy was encouraging both of them to help me. He enclosed $200 in American money that he had gotten for the lenses.

My spirits were lifted to great heights just at the thought of going to the United States. Now that somebody had agreed to sponsor me, it really seemed a reality. It was a miracle to me.

I told Ellie immediately. We were both very excited. Each day was another day of anxious anticipation. When will I hear from Mr. Schweitzer? How soon will I be permitted to leave? Will there be anything to stop me from going? My head was constantly swimming.

Several of my friends from after the war had already emigrated to America. Leon and Eva Kruger, Herschel and Ann Menche,

Der Oberstaatsanwalt
2 KMs 1/50

Wiesbaden, den 22. April 1950
Fernruf: 59321

Herrn
Abram K o r n
1727 Starnes Street
Augusta, Georgia USA

Auf das Schreiben vom 15. April 1950:

Brandscheid wurde am 28. Februar 1950 von der 2. Strafkammer
des Landgerichts Wiesbaden zu 1 Jahr 4 Monaten Gefängnis ver-
urteilt. Die Strafe ist noch nicht rechtskräftig, da Brandscheid
Revision eingelegt hat.

Im Auftrage:
gez. F l i c k
Erster Staatsanwalt

Beglaubigt:
Justizangestellte

This court document states the conviction and sixteen-month sentence of Philip Brandscheid, the guard who beat Abe with his cane at Camp Hardt.

Left to right, Billy Schweitzer, William Schweitzer, and Abe. The Schweitzer family sponsored Abe to emigrate to America in 1949.

Abe and Ellie on their wedding day in Wetzlar,
1949.

Abe and Jack Y. Platzblatt, to whom Abe dedicated
the book. Jack and Agnes Platzblatt gave Abe his
first permanent job in America.

and Simek Kirstein—friends I had lived with in Wetzlar—all had left by now. We had had many good times together, rebuilding our lives after the war. I looked forward to joining them in America.

Early in 1949, I received a letter from the American Consulate. They were working on a visa for me, it said, and I would hear from them soon. My future was slowly materializing in the direction I wanted it to go. A few weeks later I received another letter from the consulate directing me to report to Butzbach, Germany, for interrogation and a physical examination.

They interrogated me at length, and came up with no problems. My record had no blemish, and I met all the qualifications necessary to go to the United States. I also passed my physical examination on the same day. I was ecstatic. All I had to do was wait for my visa and departure date.

Ellie and I began to take the necessary steps. We set our wedding date and immediately went to Ellie's house to discuss it with her parents. They consented to the marriage wholeheartedly. They said they would make all the preparations for the wedding. Ellie's parents were happy for us, but they were sad, of course, that we would be moving so far away.

There was one small detail that we hadn't taken care of. I had not told the Schweitzers that I would be marrying Ellie. I never thought things would happen this fast. We decided to wait until after I arrived in America to tell them. We felt that it would be easier to get Ellie over to America once we were married, and we didn't want to take any chances. We were a little worried about this, but felt sure that everything would work out.

We married on August 6, 1949, just as we had planned. My old friend, Joe Grosnacht, was the best man. It was a small wedding, but very nice. Ellie was so beautiful. I will never forget how she looked that day, holding a large bouquet of flowers. It was the happiest day of my life.

We counted the days until my departure date in the fall of 1949. I would be leaving on the SS *Ellington* out of the port of Bremerhaven, Germany, en route to New Orleans, Louisiana.

When I finally received the exact time and date to be in

Bremerhaven, Ellie helped me pack for the trip. She also helped to prepare me mentally; she assured me that everything would be fine and that she would join me soon in the United States.

A few days later, I boarded a train on my way to the port city of Bremerhaven. I met a mixture of people there from all nationalities and backgrounds. We were there for three days before we boarded the steamship, the SS *General Ellington.*

This was my first journey on a seagoing vessel. I was quite excited, but also anxious. I kept thinking about my past, and worrying about my future. After all, I was on my way to a strange country, to which I hoped that I could adapt easily—not only to the people but also to the new way of life. What worried me most was that I could speak hardly any English, and that I would be completely dependent on the generous people, William and Elizabeth Schweitzer, for a full year.

After ten days' journey, we arrived in New Orleans. As the boat was docking, my excitement was indescribable. I could not have pictured in any way what I was about to see. We were told in German what to do when we would finally leave the boat. We were divided into groups by religion and were told that we would each be met by representatives of our religion.

As we left the boat, they raised the American flag. Several high school bands waited to greet us. There are no words to describe the way I felt when these bands welcomed us with the American National Anthem. They made me feel so important.

After leaving the boat, some of us were taken by cars to the Jewish Community Center in New Orleans. The wonderful people there fed us and tried to converse with us, but I could hardly understand anything they said. Our new hosts gave us moral support, and I really felt that I was among friends. I couldn't believe the overwhelming hospitality they showed us.

I don't believe anyone who didn't go through the same experiences could understand the way my friends and I felt. For years, I had been told that I was not fit to be part of society. Now I was told that my opportunities were unlimited here in America. It was up to me to learn to adapt to a new way of life and to share in the advantages of being in a great big country, the U.S.A.

After spending approximately two hours with the lovely people of New Orleans, our luggage arrived from the boat. The people from the New Orleans Jewish Community Center gave me $10 in American money and rail tickets to Augusta, Georgia. They told me not to worry about a thing. They drove me to the railroad station and told me that the conductor knew that I could not speak English. He would assist me in any way he could to make sure that I arrived safely in Augusta, Georgia.

After boarding the train, I had plenty of time to think. As I sat among the other people on the train, I felt alone. I was extremely tense and somehow afraid of my future. I saw many people around me, but I was afraid to try to talk with any of them.

Finally, I started a conversation with the few words I knew in English. I told my neighbors that I was a refugee and that I was proud for the opportunity to have a new start in their great country. I also wanted them to understand that I didn't know the language.

The patience and understanding of my traveling companions put me at ease. They really tried to communicate with me. One neighbor ordered some fried chicken for me, which I had never had before. He tried to explain to me that this was a Southern dish. It was delicious. I also had, for the first time in my life, a Coca-Cola served with my meal. I have to admit that it did not taste too good to me (although I learned to enjoy it later). My neighbor had a bit of a smile on his face when he realized that I had hardly touched my drink. He looked at me, smiled, and said, "No good?"

I looked at him and told him, "No good."

He then asked me if I wanted coffee. I told him no. I asked if I could have tea. He nodded his head and ordered tea for me. To my surprise, I was served a tall glass of iced tea, which I had never had before. We only drank hot tea at home. I thought that was what I had ordered. Since I had a hard time making myself understood, I felt that I would be better off drinking the cold tea. I smiled at my neighbor, who so generously and patiently tried to help. He even paid for everything I ordered. When I started drinking the iced tea, I loved it and still do today.

After six or seven hours, we were informed that we would soon arrive in Augusta. My heart was pounding. The only thing I knew about Augusta was that my sponsors lived there. I knew that I had to make the best out of everything. These good people, the Schweitzers, hardly even knew me. They were just doing a good deed by giving a refugee a new start in life.

After the conductor announced the arrival of the train in Augusta, he came over to me and explained that I had to leave the train. He wanted to know if he could help me to get to my destination, since he knew I did not speak English. After thanking him for his kindness, I decided that I had to start doing things for myself. I left the train.

Epilogue

My father was never able to finish his story. Even as he wrote about getting off the train in Augusta, he was already feeling the first symptoms of the disease that would quickly take his life. He wrote those last words as though he had never done anything for himself before. On the contrary, my father had always done for himself. He didn't like depending on others, or receiving handouts. Now that he had arrived in America, he was going straight to work—again.

All that my father seemed to know how to do was work. As a boy, he worked in his family's lumberyard. During the war, hard work helped to get him through the camps. After the war, he went right to work and to school, while his friends wanted to have fun and enjoy life for a change. When he came to America to build a new life with my mother, he worked hard for the rest of his life and finally reached the American Dream.

During the 1970s and 1980s, my wife, Jill, and I stayed in touch with my parents' American sponsors, the Schweitzers. We were deeply grateful for all they had done to help my parents. Mrs. Schweitzer died in 1982, and by 1987 Mr. Schweitzer was quite ill with cancer. Once a strong, vibrant man, Mr. Schweitzer was no longer able to care for himself, and he missed his wife desperately. He had lost much weight, with his trousers obviously several sizes too large. Though he was extremely weak, his mind was sharp, full of minute details. We asked him to tell us how he had helped my parents come over to America.

Happily, he shared his story with us. "When my son, Billy,

and my wife came back from a trip to Germany in 1948, Billy told me he had met a young Jewish man who wanted to come over to America. Billy asked if I would sponsor him, and I agreed. I hired a Jewish lawyer, and we sent the papers over for Abe's immigration. He arrived in 1949, without any delays. We didn't know that Abe had married Ellie until after his arrival in Augusta. That was a real surprise! So we had to get her over here, too. I went to an immigration clerk, who was also Jewish. She was very helpful, until she learned that Ellie wasn't Jewish. After that, she didn't want to help anymore. She delayed the process for almost a year."

"So how did you finally get her over?" I asked.

"In 1950, my wife and I went back to Germany to visit our family," he continued. "One morning, we went with your mother to the American Consulate in Frankfurt. The gentleman in the emigration office said that he was not the man to help us. He was the emigration clerk's supervisor and was sitting in while the clerk was out on unexpected personal business. He told us that we'd have to come back the next day.

"As we were preparing to leave, the supervisor asked us where we were from. When we told him Augusta, Georgia, a big smile came on his face, and he said, 'Well, how is J. B. White's doing?' He had recently visited Augusta and was impressed by the large department store called J. B. White's. That started a very friendly conversation." Mr. Schweitzer smiled and seemed to feel better just telling us this story.

"Because of this connection, the supervisor was very interested in helping us. He gave us some papers and pushed through the typical emigration process. Before we arrived home from Germany, Ellie was already there! We were lucky the supervisor happened to be there that day. The emigration clerk, who would normally have helped us, was known to be slow in processing emigration requests."

Mr. Schweitzer soon began to tire, and we decided that it was time to go. Sadly, he died just two weeks later, and we never got the chance to continue our talk with him.

Years later Bill Schweitzer, William's son, invited my brother, sister, and me to hear his stories about my father when he first came to America. "There are things I want to tell you about Abe that no one else knows. You better come over while I can still tell you about them." Bill's health was also failing. A recent stroke had left him partially paralyzed. Although he had a difficult time getting his words out, he knew exactly what he wanted to say.

We asked Bill how he felt when he learned that Dad had gotten married in Germany. "That was a big shock when Abe told us that he had a wife," Bill told us. "He had never mentioned anything about a wife before he came over. The feeling around my house was, 'Oh hell, what have we gotten ourselves into now!'"

Dad had worked for the Schweitzers during his first year in America. He lived with Bill and his wife, Leona, in a small garage apartment on Starnes Street in Augusta. (Later, Jill's and my first home would be on Starnes Street. We had no idea Dad had lived in that neighborhood when we bought the house.)

"Your father used to drive me crazy!" Bill told us, as he struggled physically to share his memories. "I had a short fuse when I was young, and I lost my temper with Abe many times. One of the things that used to get me fuming mad was when he would take a bath. He used to fill up that tub, and it seemed that he would stay in there for hours! We only had one bathroom."

"Yes," I said, "Dad even wrote about enjoying his baths. Can you imagine how good it must have felt for him to take a bath after living in filth for so many years, unable to really bathe at all?"

"You know," Bill replied, "I never looked at it that way. I guess you're right."

We left Bill's house with a few more pieces of the puzzle.

In 1985, already ill with her own fatal disease, my mother shared with me the memories of her and Dad's first years together in America.

"When I came over in 1950," Mom told me, "your father had almost completed his one-year responsibility to work for the Schweitzers. He greatly appreciated what the Schweitzers had done for him, but it was important to Abe to get a job on his own merits. He'd had several temporary jobs until he set out with a friend to find his first real job in America. They walked up and down Broad Street, visiting the many Jewish merchants downtown. When they walked into Agnes Auto Parts, Jack and Agnes Platzblatt gave him his first job. Abe was a tiny man who could hardly speak English, but 'Mr. Jack' and 'Aggie' saw something in Abe that they liked. They wanted to help him.

"Mr. Jack was hard on your father," Mom continued. "He was a gruff man, always cussing and yelling. Jack often pushed Abe to the limit in their years working together, and I would have to calm him down when he came home. As hard as Mr. Jack was on the surface, he had a heart of gold. He and Aggie loved us, and we loved them. They took us in as their own family.

"When Aggie learned that Abe and I were living with Billy and his wife in that little garage apartment, she said, 'That's no place to raise a family. We're moving to a new home very soon. You will live in our old home when we move.' So it was."

Like my parents, I loved the Platzblatts. Mr. Jack and Aggie never had children, and, when I was born, they considered me their first grandchild. Aggie and I had a special relationship, and I'll never forget the love we had for each other. She was the kindest person I ever knew. When my brother and sister were born, they took new delight in each of them. The Platzblatts finally had a family of their own to love.

Jack was a real business entrepreneur. He loved to get out and sell. He bought everything he could get his hands on during the war, including watches, radios, televisions, and washing machines. After the war, his business was one of the few that had much of anything to sell. People still come up to me today and say, "I got my first television from Jack Platzblatt." Jack was the salesman, always selling something or giving it away, and Aggie was the storekeeper.

Dad started out cleaning the store and delivering parts on a bicycle. He soon learned the parts business and helped manage the store. He worked day and night, and played a major role in the tremendous success of the business. They had started out as a little auto parts and tire shop and, with Dad's help, soon outgrew their downtown location. In 1955 they closed Agnes Auto Parts and opened Parts Warehouse Company in a much larger building, selling only to auto parts stores. As a wholesaler of auto parts, they helped many small businesses get started in the Augusta area, often financing their initial inventories.

One of Dad's former customers, Harold Mays, recalled how my father was respected in the business community. "Abe would have been a tremendous success at any business he would have gone into," Harold said. "He had a head for numbers and an incredible memory. He understood inventory control and all aspects of running a business. On top of that, he was a workaholic. Most important, he had a winning way with people. He could take more abuse than anybody I knew and still not lose his temper with the customers. He loved people." Undoubtedly, Dad's experience in the concentration camps made dealing with disgruntled customers seem almost effortless.

By all means he was a workaholic. He worked hard all day and almost always came home late. After dinner and a short break to be with the family and watch the news, Dad would pull out trays full of inventory cards and begin ordering merchandise, often working late into the night. When he had free time, he was working around the house or helping a friend with an electrical problem, putting his training as an electrical engineer to good use.

Dad also enjoyed working in the yard, planting shrubs and trees. He liked their permanence. I remember walking in the woods with Dad, looking for tiny cedar seedlings. We dug up several and planted them in our back yard, thinking they would grow into large bushes. They are now more than thirty feet tall, and I had to cut several of them down, years ago, so that the others would have room to grow.

On weekends, we kids would go to a nearby lake, Clark's Hill, with Aggie and Mom. Dad would always show up late in the afternoon, with double the usual amount of inventory cards to go through. We swam, boated, and fished, while Dad worked. He hated to waste time, but he did enjoy getting out in the boat.

Dad soon became general manager of the business, which continued to grow rapidly under his leadership. Jack spent more time on the road, and Aggie began to take life a little easier. When Jack died in 1962,[1] Aggie appointed Dad to the position of vice-president. He was so proud. He was soon in full charge as president, as Aggie began thinking of retirement. She had complete trust and faith in my father.

Not only did Dad continue Jack's practice of helping new customers get started in business, but he also assisted his employees in buying new homes and new cars. He wanted to help them improve their lives. It seems everyone loved my father—his customers, his employees, his suppliers, his friends. They knew him to be fair and honest and always helping others. "Gentle" is the word I hear most commonly to describe him. Dad truly was a gentle man.

In 1965—sixteen years after Dad had come to America with nothing but his desire to be successful—my parents were finally able to build their dream home. Dad had been told that if he worked hard enough in America, he could accomplish anything. Aggie moved into a new home after Jack died, and Dad bought the property across the street from her. There we built a beautiful, two-story brick home and could still be near Aggie. Dad's new home was a symbol of his success. My own family lives there today.

Besides building his own house, Dad always dreamed that the business he loved would be his. He had worked hard for the Platzblatts for many years, and now Aggie was losing a long battle with cancer. In 1971, when she finally succumbed, Aggie left Parts Warehouse Company to Dad in her will. It was a mixed blessing. He was deeply saddened to lose Aggie, who had been like a mother to him and Mom, but now he had achieved his long-time goal of owning the business. Honored that she would bequeath it to him, Dad was finally the proud owner of Parts Warehouse Company.

---

1. Two years before Abe became vice-president, the Eichmann trial, in Jerusalem, was broadcast all over the world. Adolf Eichmann, who oversaw the expulsions of Jews from Greater Germany and the transport of Jews to ghettos, concentration camps, and death camps, was found guilty and sentenced to death.

Dad could only bask in the glory for a very short time. He had worked for more than twenty years to achieve this dream, and he died just fifteen months later.

Mom came into the business for the first time in her life. As the new president, she rapidly learned the business and grew to be widely respected. She even served as the first woman on the board of governors of a major industry trade association. My brother and I grew up in the business and always planned to enter it when we got out of school. When our sister, Helen, graduated from college in 1983, I even sold her on the idea of joining us to continue our family heritage. Our mother died in 1985. My brother, my sister, and I continued to run the business. We worked together amazingly well, as our parents had taught us to put family first.

In my mother's last year on earth, we decided to open our first retail auto parts store. Mom was so excited as we made plans for the new store. She died on May 26, 1985, five days before our planned grand opening. We wondered if we should delay the opening celebration. Our rabbi encouraged us to go on with the opening, in Mom's honor. So, on May 31, Aggie's birthday, we held our "grand re-opening" celebration of Agnes Auto Parts.

Several years later, I received a phone call from the manager of that store. A man had come in to speak to me, and the manager put him on the phone. "Hi, I'm Tom McEntire. I noticed the name of this store and knew you had to be one of the Korns. I knew your parents from way back. We used to live in Augusta, but now we own a country inn in the mountains. Why don't you come see us? My wife and I would love to meet you and your family, and we have an amazing story to tell you about your father." Tom left his card, and although we called them a couple of times, it wasn't until years later, after we sold the business, that Jill and I finally made our visit.

After finally creating the time to work on the book, my wife and I wanted to learn as much as we could about my father. When we visited the McEntires in January 1993, Jill and I couldn't wait to hear what they had to tell us.

"I grew up outside of Augusta," Tom began, "and lived there for most of my life. Mary and I used to go to a public lake across the South Carolina border. I think it was called Yonce Lake. We were sitting there on the beach one day, in 1952, enjoying the sun and the water, when I noticed a man staring at us. I wondered what such a funny-looking little man was doing with a taller, beautiful blonde. It bothered me because every time I looked over, this man was staring at me. We finally picked up our towels and chairs and moved to a different place on the beach. This guy got up and starting walking toward us.

"I was very nervous when he walked up. He came up to me and asked, 'Were you a *Panzer?*'

"'Yes,' I said, 'I drove a tank in the war.'

"'Buchenwald?' he asked.

"'Yeah,' I said, 'I went to Buchenwald.'

"'I was there.'

"'What do you mean—you were there?' I said, more than a little stunned.

"'I was at Buchenwald. You gave me a candy bar and then took it away from me.'

"Then I knew what he meant," Tom told us. "I was in a U.S. Army tank unit in the war, the 737th Tank Battalion. They called us 'Patton's Spearheaders.' We had stormed the beaches at Normandy, had fought in the Battle of the Bulge, and were liberating villages in Germany. I had been drinking a little too much when they asked for volunteers to go into Buchenwald, so I volunteered. Well, I can tell you now, that was the first and last time I ever volunteered for anything in the army!

"I knew that Buchenwald was a concentration camp, but I didn't really know what a concentration camp was. In my mind, they were like prisoner-of-war camps. I had no idea what I was in for. We had heard rumors, but didn't really believe them.

"We went through the gates, and I'll never forget what I saw inside those walls. The first thing I noticed was an incredible stench. Corpses were piled up everywhere, like cordwood. Even children were in those piles. Once you smell that smell, of decaying bodies, you'll never forget it. I couldn't handle it, and I vomited.

"When I felt a little better, I wanted to help the people

there. They were so weak. They looked like walking skeletons, barely alive. I handed out about six D-bars, army-issue chocolate bars, almost 100 percent pure chocolate. After I gave them out, a medic told me to take them back, that the chocolate might kill them. It was too rich for their starved bodies. I hated to, but I started taking them back from those poor, starving people. They fought me like cats, kicking and biting me, but I got most of the chocolate back.

"That's how Abe remembered me. He was one of them. He had only seen me that one time, about seven years before that day at the lake. I couldn't believe it.

"When I explained it to Mary, she was as amazed as I was. We were both stunned. It was the eeriest thing that we had ever experienced. It sent chills through us from head to toe.

"Then Ellie walked up, and we sat and talked together all afternoon. We enjoyed each other's company so much that we became fast friends. I never understood how Abe remembered me after all those years. I still can hardly believe it, even as I'm sitting here telling you the story."

"I think I understand," I said. "Dad always had an excellent memory. Mom used to say he had a photographic memory. When he was in the camps, he had been praying for liberation for years. As the American army approached, Dad could hardly believe that he was about to be liberated. When you and your fellow soldiers finally arrived, with your tanks and camouflage uniforms and bayonets, you were real heroes to Dad and to the rest of the survivors. When you gave him a chocolate bar, and then took it away, your face was burned into his memory forever. Fate brought you together again, thousands of miles away and many years later, and he remembered you."

"Your father was an incredible man," Tom told me. "He was an incredible man."

Afterword

I was only 19 when I learned that my father was dying of a rare and incurable disease. The doctors couldn't tell us much about the illness. At first they thought it was tuberculosis, possibly a carryover from his days in concentration camps, but the doctors soon ruled that out. Finally, they called it diffuse pulmonary interstitial fibrosis—a name that merely described the symptoms. The doctors didn't know what caused his disease, nor did they know how to treat it. All they could tell us was that he would die of suffocation very soon. What the Nazis couldn't do in more than five years, fate would take care of in a few short months.

I did much thinking in those last few months before my father died. Dad meant more to me than anyone else in the world. I remember sitting in the hospital waiting room in the last days—a thousand thoughts racing through my mind. Why is he dying? Why haven't I been closer to him? Why haven't I spent more time with him? Why didn't I go to Israel with him when he wanted me to? Why didn't I learn more about him? Why? Why? Why!

I guess I was as close to my father as the average American teenager—too busy trying to fit in with other teenagers to really get to know him—but that wasn't enough. My father was dying, and my world was collapsing around me.

I loved him so much, but I hadn't told him that in years, because I was "too big" for all of that. Now, more than anything, I wanted to tell Dad that I loved him, and I wasn't even sure that he would know I was there.

I walked into the room. Dad was a pitiful sight. Under an oxygen tent, his body was extremely thin, with tubes sticking in his arms, chest, and nose. He had cuts all over from the many biopsies the doctors had performed to study the disease. He was breathing hard, but very little oxygen was getting into his bloodstream. He hadn't responded to us in days. He looked much like he must have looked after liberation from the concentration camps—only a shell of a human being.

Amazingly, he looked up and recognized me. Now was my chance, but I couldn't get the words out of my mouth. They were pounding in my consciousness—I LOVE YOU! I LOVE YOU! I LOVE YOU! They stayed locked inside until I was about to explode. Why couldn't I get them out? Finally, I said it. "I love you, Dad." After all that agonizing, the words seemed so easy to say as they softly left my lips. He heard—and he understood.

"I love you, too, son," he whispered as he squeezed my hand and looked at me through the transparent wall of the oxygen tent. That moment felt so good. He died just a few hours later. There were a million things that I wished I had said to him and done with him. At least, I had told him that I loved him.

My father was able to leave the Nazi concentration camps, but the memories never left him. He tried to block them out, but couldn't. Many years after the war, they would still come to the surface in his dreams. I remember waking to his screams in the night; I knew that he'd had another nightmare. My mother, my brother, my sister, and I would be in the camps with him in those terrifying dreams. My father suffered with insomnia for all of his adult life. As much as he wanted to sleep, he was afraid he would wake up back in the camps.

Even though Dad did talk to Mom and his friends about his experiences in the camps, he simply couldn't talk to us, his children, about it very much. If we would ask him a question, he would give a short answer and that would be all. It was just too difficult for him.

Dad started writing his memoirs in 1969, twenty-four years after his liberation. He would meet as often as he could with a friend, Jack Wyland. Often our rabbi, Benjamin Rosayn, would join them. Jack had been trying to get Dad to write his story for many years, and he had finally convinced him. Writing his memoirs was like therapy for my father. Finally he could release what had been locked inside for most of his life. He began to sleep better; the nightmares began to subside. He began to live easier.

Dad and Jack would try to meet on Thursday nights to work on the book, but sometimes would skip months at a time. Dad would tell his story, and they either recorded the sessions on tape or wrote them out. Another friend, Mary Lou Helmly, typed them. Whatever they accomplished during one evening of work would become one chapter. Originally there were 36 chapters, representing 36 sessions. The shortest chapter was less than 3 pages long; the longest was 15. I have combined many of the chapters and separated others to end up with 18 chapters.

The numbers 18 and 36 have special meanings in the Jewish religion. *Life* in Hebrew is expressed as *Chai* and is represented by the number 18. The number 36 represents double-*Chai*. It is said that the world is perpetually sustained by 36 righteous people living on earth. When one dies, another is born. For thousands of years, the *Chai*, or 18, has been used to express our faith and prayer that the Eternal will bestow the blessing of Life upon us. My father's story is about life, not death.

On January 12, 1972, Dad met with Jack to work on Chapter 35. This was their first session in more than five months, and they were almost to the end of the story. Jack died suddenly, twelve days later. By the time Dad wrote the last chapter in late April, he was already beginning to feel the first symptoms of his illness. He died on August 7, 1972, one day after my parents' twenty-third wedding anniversary.

I had read some of Dad's manuscript as he was writing it. After he died, I began reading it several times, but never got very far into it. Several years later, as I was beginning to settle into adult life, I finally picked up the manuscript to read it from cover to cover. Reading it had a powerful impact on me. I felt closer to Dad than I ever had before, and he was no longer by my side. I began to understand what was so special about my father, and I was thankful that he had left his story for me, for my family, and for everyone else to read.

I first became interested in having *Abe's Story* published in the early 1980s, after Rabbi Chaim Wender asked me to teach a religious school class on the Holocaust. It embarrassed me to tell him that I really didn't know much about the Holocaust. Sadly, detailed information about the Holocaust wasn't taught in public schools (and still isn't, for the most part), and I didn't even learn about it in religious school. Rabbi Wender said, "You know your father's book, don't you? That's enough." I have since taught a Holocaust class to eighth- and ninth-grade students. Alternating every other year, we first read Dad's manuscript aloud, then discuss it. The second year, we read Elie Wiesel's extraordinary book, *Night*. We also discuss current events, comparing them to what happened during the Holocaust and to events in pre-war Europe.

For years, my students would ask, "When are you going to have your father's book published?"

Every year, I would reply, "Someday . . . someday I'll create the time."

That time came for me in 1993, and *Abe's Story* is the result. As editor of this tribute to my father, and to other sufferers of the Holocaust, I urge all living survivors to record their stories in whatever forms possible. World War II ended 50 years ago, and only about 350,000 survivors are still alive. They are getting old. How many will be alive in 10 years? In 20 years? In 30? All too soon, the survivors will be gone, so we must have their recorded testimonies to keep their memories alive. Whether written, filmed, or recorded electronically or on audio tape, survivors' accounts must be preserved.

I have taken Dad's purpose of recording his experiences one step further. I am joining with the continuing worldwide efforts to ensure that memories of the concentration camps stay alive, so that the world will never forget. Editing and publishing *Abe's Story* is my small way of preserving a bit of history, to remind the world of what we allowed to happen such a short time ago.

Afterword

My father continually serves as a source of inspiration for me. When I feel sorry for myself or feel depressed, I reflect on his perseverance through the Holocaust, and it lifts my spirits. I think of the struggle of so many millions of his peers.

As you come to know my father through *Abe's Story*, may you find strength to face your challenges in a new light. May we all appreciate life's blessings, great or small, and more rigorously oppose hatred and persecution around the world.

Joseph Korn

Randy Salzman

The Korn family today. All of Abe's children and grand-children still live in Augusta, Georgia.

Further Reading

History
Adult Readers

Arad, Yitzhak. *The Pictorial History of the Holocaust*. New York: Macmillan, 1990.

Bauer, Yehuda. *A History of the Holocaust*. New York: Franklin Watts, 1982.

Feig, Konnilyn. *Hitler's Death Camps*. New York: Holmes & Meier, 1979.

Flannery, Edward. *The Anguish of the Jews: Twenty-Three Centuries of Antisemitism*. New York: Paulist Press, 1985.

Gilbert, Martin. *Atlas of the Holocaust*. New York: William Morrow, 1993.

———. *The Holocaust: A History of the Jews of Europe During the Second World War*. New York: Henry Holt, 1985.

Hilberg, Raul. *The Destruction of the European Jews*. New York: Harper Torch Books, 1961.

Landau, Ronnie, *The Nazi Holocaust*. Chicago: Ivan R. Dee, 1994.

Sixth- through Twelfth-Grade Readers

Adler, David. *We Remember the Holocaust*. New York: Henry Holt and Co., 1989.

Chaiken, Miriam. *A Nightmare in History: The Holocaust 1933-1945*. Boston: Houghton Mifflin, 1987.

Meltzer, Milton, *Never to Forget: The Jews of the Holocaust*. New York: Dell Publishing Co., 1976.

Stadtler, Bea. *The Holocaust: A History of Courage and Resistance*. West Orange, N.Y.: Behrman House, 1975.

Fiction and Memoirs
Adult Readers

Epstein, Helen. *Children of the Holocaust*. New York: Penguin, 1988.

Fink, Ida. *The Journey*. New York: A Plume Book, 1990.

Hersey, John. *The Wall*. New York: Vintage Books, 1977.

Levi, Primo. *Survival in Auschwitz*. New York: Macmillan, 1961.

Pisar, Samuel. *Of Blood and Hope*. New York: Macmillan, 1980.

Weisel, Elie, *Night*. New York: Bantam, 1982.

Sixth- through Twelfth-Grade Readers

Frank, Anne. *Anne Frank: The Diary of a Young Girl*. New York: Pocket Books, 1958.

Lowry, Lois. *Number the Stars*. New York: Dell Yearling Book, 1989.

Matas, Carol. *Daniel's Story*. New York: Scholastic, 1993.

Yolan, Jane. *The Devil's Arithmetic*. New York: Penguin, 1988.

Videos

The Courage to Care. Documentary. 30 minutes. Source: Zenger Video (800-421-4246), 10200 Jefferson Blvd., Room 902, P.O. Box 802, Culver City, CA 90232-0802.

Daniel's Story. Docudrama. 14 minutes. Source: U.S. Holocaust Memorial Museum (202-488-0400), 100 Raoul Wallenberg Place, S.W., Washington, D.C. 20024-2150.

Genocide (The World at War Series, vol. 20). Documentary. 50 minutes. Source: Arts and Entertainment (800-423-1212), or A&E Home Video, P.O. Box 2284, South Burlington, VT 05407.

The Hangman. Animated. 12 minutes. Source: CRM (800-421-0833), 2215 Faraday, Suite F, Carlsbad, CA 92008.

As 1995 commemorates the 50th anniversary of the end of World War II and the 25th anniversary of Earth Day, we recognize that we each have a responsibility to build and sustain a better world. Human rights, freedom, justice, peace, and the preservation of the earth are possible and absolutely necessary to ensure a safer world for future generations. In our effort to recognize these beliefs, we have initiated a special tree-planting program.

The Korn family will also donate a portion of its profits from the sale of *Abe's Story* to Holocaust education projects.

You are invited to participate in
our **Trees for Chai** (Life)
tree-planting program.

$10 for 10 trees

Trees can be planted in memory of,
or in honor of, a person or group.

Please *print* your information on a separate sheet of paper and send with your tax-deductible check, payable to the Earth Day Alliance, to:

Trees for Chai
P.O. Box 60087
Augusta, GA 30909

Remembering the past provides a necessary foundation for envisioning the future. In 1995 and beyond, may we have vision and courage to embrace all of humanity.

Joseph and Jill Korn, 1995